The Sound of
a Silver Horn

The Sound of a Silver Horn

Reclaiming the Heroism in Contemporary Women's Lives

Kathleen Noble, Ph.D.

FAWCETT COLUMBINE • NEW YORK

Grateful acknowledgment is made to the following for permission
to reprint previously published material:

Harcourt Brace & Company, and Faber and Faber Ltd: Excerpt from "Little
Gidding" in *Four Quartets* by T. S. Eliot. Copyright 1943 by T. S. Eliot and
renewed 1971 by Esme Valerie Eliot. Reprinted by permission of Harcourt
Brace & Company and Faber and Faber Ltd.

Alfred A. Knopf, Inc.: Excerpt from "Madman's Song" from *The Collected
Poems of Elinor Wylie* by Elinor Wylie. Copyright 1932 by Alfred A. Knopf,
Inc. and renewed 1960 by Edwina C. Rubenstein. Reprinted by permission
of the publisher.

W. W. Norton & Company, Inc.: Excerpt from "Prospective Immigrants
Please Note" from *Collected Early Poems, 1950–1970*, by Adrienne Rich.
Copyright © 1993 by Adrienne Rich. Copyright © 1967, 1963, 1962, 1961,
1960, 1959, 1958, 1957, 1956, 1955, 1954, 1953, 1952, 1951 by Adrienne Rich.
Copyright © 1984, 1975, 1971, 1969, 1966 by W. W. Norton & Company, Inc.
Reprinted by permission of the author and W. W. Norton & Company, Inc.

LIBRARY OF CONGRESS CATALOGING-IN-PUBLICATION DATA
Noble, Kathleen.
The sound of a silver horn: reclaiming the heroism in
contemporary women's lives / Kathleen Noble. — 1st ed.
p. cm.
ISBN 0-449-90588-8
1. Women—Psychology. 2. Heroines. 3. Women—Mythology.
4. Feminist criticism. I. Title.
HQ1206.N68 1994
305.42—dc20   93-14264
CIP

Text design by Holly Johnson

Cover design by Georgia Morrissey

Cover illustration by Brad Teare

Manufactured in the United States of America

First Edition: March 1994

10 9 8 7 6 5 4 3 2 1

For Rose, my Ally, Friend, and Mentor,
Who helped me see that everything is truly a grace.

"Better to see your cheek grown hollow,
Better to see your temple torn,
Than to forget to follow, follow,
After the sound of a silver horn."

ELINOR WYLIE
"MADMAN'S SONG,"
COLLECTED POEMS, 1932

Contents

Acknowledgments

One afternoon in February 1988, I walked into the office of a colleague who greeted me with what I thought was a peculiar question. "How does it feel to be in vogue?" she asked, with a huge grin on her face. Bewildered, I looked at my T-shirt and faded jeans and wondered what the punch line of her joke would be. "No," she said, "I mean, how does it feel to be in *Vogue* magazine?" I had no idea what she was talking about until she told me that a scholarly article of mine, entitled "The Dilemma of the Gifted Woman," had been excerpted in that month's edition of *Vogue*.

I was even more astonished when I arrived at my office later that week and answered a call from literary agent Felicia Eth, who had read this same excerpt and wondered whether I might be interested in writing a book. I had been considering the idea for some time, I said, but I didn't know where to start or whether I could do it. Felicia listened with the good humor of one who has worked with many fledgling authors. "Of course you can do it," she said, and she would help me bring the book to birth. The idea took shape slowly, but a year after our first conversation I knew the direction in which I would head. When Joanne Wyckoff became my editor at Ballantine Books, the quest began in earnest.

Many allies have guided me throughout this adventure, and I would like to publicly and gratefully acknowledge their assistance. Felicia and Joanne have been the most remarkable gifts; I feel very privileged to have had access not only to their consummate literary skills but to their warmth, friendship, and encouragement. Linda Silverman befriended me at a turning point in my life and encouraged my interest in working with gifted women, a direction that was integral to the evolution of this book. She and Constance Hollinger were the anonymous reviewers who eagerly accepted "The Dilemma of the Gifted Woman" for publication in *Psychology of Women Quarterly* and unwittingly set this quest in motion. I am grateful for their confidence and support, then and now.

A year after "The Dilemma . . ." was published it metamorphosed into a speech about female heroism, due in part to the work of Carol Pearson and Katherine Pope, to which I was introduced by Pat Lake. Mona Murr Kunselman insisted that I turn the speech into a publication, and the editors and reviewers of *Women and Therapy* received it with an enthusiasm that buoyed my confidence and gave me the courage I needed to build this book upon its foundation.

Janyce Imig, Gloria Koepping, Priscilla Wright, and Anne Wiedenfeld, colleagues in my peer consultation group, were supportive from the beginning. Janyce, Gloria, Brenda Bankhead, Hollis Giammatteo, Margie Hattori, Mary Lewis, and Rita Coburn Whack critiqued the work as it progressed and persuaded me to tell some stories I would otherwise have been reluctant to share. Don Middendorf helped me keep the work tied always to its larger vision. David Regal offered his analytic skills whenever I foundered and made sure I took periodic vacations to replenish my psyche. Cecile Andrews, Stephanie Bravmann, Janice Fournier, Lisa Giles, Susan Gunderson, Dave Kirdahy, Mona Murr and John Kunselman, Susan Lillich, Erina MacGeorge, David Mitchell, and Kelli Jayn Nichols cheered me on as I approached each hurdle and reminded me that the work was worthwhile when my confidence waned. Sue Andrina voluntarily transcribed hours of interviews, saving me an enormous amount of energy and time.

Nancy Robinson also gave me a great gift of time. She released me periodically from my responsibilities at the University of Washington and made it possible for me to concentrate exclusively on the book when I most needed to do so. She, Ellen Mosolf, Kay Soberg, and the faculty and staff of the Halbert Robinson Center for the Study of Capable Youth patiently endured my agonies and ecstasies as I plowed my way through the writing process. My students fueled me with their laughter, humor, and unquenchable idealism and always reminded me of what was truly important in life. The Honeybear Bakery nourished me with copious quantities of cafe latte, "Chelan Sunrise," and peanut butter cookies and provided a congenial place to write for hours.

I especially want to acknowledge the women who entrusted me with their stories for this book, and the clients who entrusted me with their lives, all of whom must remain anonymous. I have learned more from them about the reality of heroism, healing, and wholeness than one book could ever contain, and I have deepened and matured as a result of their tutelage.

I also wish to thank Nancy Skinner Nordhoff for creating Cottages at Hedgebrook, an enchanted retreat for women writers on Whidbey Island, Washington, which is overseen by herself and several other guiding spirits: Denise Anderson, Kathleen Baginski, Connie Brotherton, Holly Gault, Linda Haverfield, Ken McElroy, Gene McJunkin, and Jennifer Rose. Hedgebrook was an extraordinary gift of time, solitude, and community with other writers. I did some of my best thinking, feeling, and writing there, laughed and cried in equal proportions, and ate some of the finest meals I've had in years, all in the company of my sister writers Brenda Bankhead, Jean Bryant, Hollis Giammatteo, Margie Hattori, Mary Lewis, and Rita Coburn Whack. Tillie Olsen, who was leaving Hedgebrook as I arrived, introduced me to the poetry of Elinor Wylie, wherein I found the book's title. To all these women I give my deepest and most heartfelt appreciation. It is no exaggeration to say that this book would have suffered immeasurably had I not had the privilege of a residency at Hedgebrook.

I have stood on the shoulders of many women who have gone before in order to write this book. I had planned to speak through a more objective, impersonal voice until I read the words of Carolyn Heilbrun and Carol Christ, entreating women to tell our stories "profoundly," and took them to heart. Rose Marie Robertson taught me much about being both a writer and a fully human being and inspired me with her own example. To all the mothers who have opened doors through which I have been able to walk, to all the women who will open doors for generations of people to come, thank you, and Godspeed.

The Sound of
a Silver Horn

Introduction

Several years ago I was preparing a closing address for a conference of highly capable women and looking for a metaphor that would spark my listeners' imaginations. As I thought about the issues women face in their lives, my attention was drawn to the popular literature then being published for and about women. I was distressed to discover many bestselling books describing us as loving too much, making foolish choices, and exhibiting a wide variety of self-destructive complexes. Even my own previous writing, I realized with dismay, had focused more on our problems than on our strengths. While I do not wish to disparage this literature in its entirety, it became clear to me that we are cast—and often cast ourselves—in the role of tragic "heroine," rather than in a paradigm that would galvanize our energies and significantly enhance our efficacy in the world.

As I wove these perceptions into my address I decided to build a different model, one that reflected not only the struggle but the excitement and joy of wielding our deepest potentials. Because I had always been fascinated by the idea and the ideal of the heroic quest, I wanted to see how women's lives would look through its unique lens. First, though, I had to choose the word to describe a woman who embarked upon this quest. *Heroine?* Although it denoted the female member of a heroic drama, I never liked the word, though I wasn't sure why. *Hero?* That sounded too masculine, too "Herculean" for my taste. *Female hero?* Literary scholars Carol Pearson and Katherine Pope[1] had used the term in the title of their book about adventurous women in American and British literature. It struck a hopeful chord.

I turned to my students, colleagues, and friends for help in resolving this dilemma. What did the word *heroine* mean to them? Most laughed or grimaced and conjured up images of modest maidens hoping their princes would arrive, or hapless females tied to railroad tracks waiting for heroes to charge to their rescue. Of course, many added, a heroine was supposed to be beautiful and kind, as well as generous, unselfish, and good. "Well, doesn't she perform any great deeds?" I inquired. The women looked pensive and said that if she did, they went largely unnoticed or were rarely significant.

When I asked what impressions the word *hero* evoked, their responses were more immediate and assured. Heroes were brave, adventurous men who risked their lives to perform daring acts of discovery or rescue for the good of mankind. "Must they be handsome?" I always asked. While heroes were supposed to be intelligent and strong, and willing to face anything that threatened the tasks they had set for themselves, physical attractiveness was the least of the virtues required.

Finally I asked my informants about female heroes. Could they name any women who exemplified the qualities they had just ascribed to male heroes? At this point many looked perplexed and, after a silence, mentioned only one or two, like Eleanor Roosevelt or Joan of Arc. Why was it difficult to identify heroic women? Part of the problem, I believe, lies in the word we use, because words have tremendous power to constrict or enlarge our ideas about people and their possibilities. The word *heroine*, as it has been defined and used historically, does not begin to describe the many women who live lives of courage, strength, initiative, and independence. Most heroic myths celebrate these qualities only in men, and as a result many people believe that women are not heroic or are unique or deviant if they strive to be so.

From medieval legends of El Cid and King Arthur to contemporary stories of Batman and Bruce Lee, popular tales portray male heroes as exceptional people who epitomize the greatest attributes and aspirations of men. These archetypal heroes are usually successful warriors who display superior strength and courage, or men who wield social, political, or spiritual power. The hero gives shape to himself, and he lives life on his own terms regardless of cost. Historically heroes have been revered for their great capacity for life and for pursuing "higher goals." They are expected to develop their resilience, autonomy, and self-reliance, to approach the challenges in their lives with intelligence and creativity, and to act with integrity in all endeavors. Their quests challenge them to roam the inner or outer worlds in search of new knowledge and to use that knowledge to serve their fellow creatures. He who seeks the Grail, the mysterious core of each mythic journey, is the quintessential hero, even if he perishes in the process.

But what about heroines? Although a male hero is *always* defined in terms of his quest, a heroine typically is defined by her gender or support roles. While the hero develops his greatest potential, in story after story the heroine cultivates her beauty and purity, sublimates her desire for autonomy, growth, and adventure, and finds her identity through her relationship with a man. Though the heroine is stereotyped by qualities of appearance and virtue that real women never possess, she represents the highest ideal toward which women strive. But she is an ideal who languishes in castles or on railroad tracks waiting to be rescued, and once rescued gives up her self for those whom she loves. In virtually all heroic tales the man takes the active, assertive role while the woman is passive, the prize to be won or fought over, the maiden in distress. And regardless of the outcome of his quest, the hero takes the heroine with him or leaves her to a tragic fate.

From ancient times the heroine has been consistently drawn as a gentle, quiet, and unassuming female.

She applies herself diligently to all of her tasks and is content to remain within the sphere of her home, obedient to the authority of fathers, husbands, or brothers. She never argues or expresses strong emotions other than love, and she never challenges the misogynistic sentiments propounded all around her—in law, literature, philosophy, religion, and social mores. If she does defy this "natural order" and attempt to live autonomously, to assert her power or eschew the limits imposed upon her gender, she is castigated as a dangerous, unfeminine, and contemptible being whose actions will lead to the destruction of society and universal chaos.

This dynamic is clearly evident in Greek mythology, from which many of Western civilization's most cherished, potent, and enduring symbols of heroism derive. The ancient Greeks gave us no female character equal to the stature of Heracles, Prometheus, or Achilles, because only men were thought to be the bearers of culture.[2] Instead, some of their most memorable females, such as Circe, Medusa, and the Furies, were portrayed as monsters whom mortal men must vanquish in order to attain their heroic stature. Women who were celebrated as heroines in Greek literature achieved that status largely through self-sacrifice or martyrdom. Iphegenia, for example, dutifully acquiesced to her father's decision to sacrifice her to the gods so that the success of his mission might be assured. It was, she said, "better that one man live to see the light of day than ten thousand women."[3] Women who refused to be docile or submissive were censured for their assertive, unfeminine, and wicked behavior. Such was Medea's fate when she exacted a terrible revenge upon her unfaithful husband, Jason, for deserting her and her children after she saved his life and helped him win the Golden Fleece. Both gods and goddesses in Greek mythology frequently set heroic tasks for mortal men to achieve, but goddesses, subordinate to the gods and significantly less powerful, never exhorted women to develop their heroic potential. Rather, as historian Sarah Pomeroy discovered, goddesses were "hostile to women, or [were shown] pursuing many activities foreign to the experience of mortal women."[4]

Heroines fared no better in the creation myths of the ancient Hebrews, whose early writings, along with those of the Greeks and Romans, form "the matrix of later European culture."[5] Lilith and Eve, the principal female characters in this literature, are the prototypes from which all subsequent heroines are drawn. Lilith was purported to be the first woman, created simultaneously with Adam to be his wife and helpmate. But she refused to be subordinate and left him, thereafter to be maligned as a temptress, a menace to children, and the incarnation of evil. Lilith was succeeded by Eve, who became the mother of Adam's children and, by extension, the mother of all human beings. But Eve also suffered under the Hebraic hand; rather than submit to ignorance in the Garden of Eden, she chose to listen to the serpent, the prepatriarchal symbol of the Goddess. Her punishment for this act of disobedience was banishment from Paradise, pain in childbirth, and submission to the authority of men, which was "divinely decreed . . . at the very dawn of existence."[6]

European romance stories, poems, and songs from the twelfth through fifteenth centuries calcified the image of the heroine through a meticulously drawn code of chivalry and courtly love. Once again, in tales such as "Beowulf," "Tristan and Isolde," and "Le Morte d'Arthur," women were idealized for their modesty, beauty, chastity, piety, obedience, and selfless performance of domestic duties. When the praises of these heroines were sung by medieval troubadours it was not because of any brave deeds they had performed, but for maintaining their loyalty and virtue in the face of whatever temptations or misfortunes had befallen them.

Heroines like Guinevere and Isolde may have been seen as objects of love, but as historians Bonnie Anderson and Judith Zinsser point out, "love, not the woman herself, caused the hero to act, to test and prove himself."[7] These stories and songs cast women in a heinous double bind. Although love for a woman could ennoble a man, it could also turn him into a fool or a murderer, cause him to completely forget himself and his obligations or, like Lancelot, to break his vow of chastity and become ineligible to complete his heroic quest. Thus, however virtuous women might appear, they were also daughters of the biblical Eve and the Greek Pandora: by nature treacherous, duplicitous, lascivious, and unpredictable, able to ruin the best of men if not held firmly in check by stringent codes of behavior and morality.

The mythology of the heroine was further crystal-
lized in the character of "patient Griselda," the Renaissance exemplar of the perfect wife, and of "Sleeping
Beauty," the seventeenth-century guide for young women
aspiring to a place in the French court. Its hold on the
popular imagination was reinforced by the fairy tales of
the Brothers Grimm and Hans Christian Andersen, stories that gained widespread appeal in our own time
through the animation of Walt Disney. Folklorist Kay
Stone has said that although heroines appear in 40 of the
210 stories that make up the Grimm Brothers' collec-
tion, "[v]ery few translations offer more than 25 tales,
and thus only a handful of heroines is usually included.
Most of them run the gamut from mildly abused to se-
verely persecuted. In fact, a dozen docile heroines are the
overwhelming favorites, reappearing in book after book
from the mid-19th century to the present."[8]

Today, films are powerful purveyors of cultural attitudes and mores and are dominated by stories about
men and boys who embark upon various quests while
women wait patiently for their attention, living their
lives in the shadows cast by male adventure. Consider,
for example, *Crocodile Dundee*, the Indiana Jones mov-
ies, and *Beverly Hills Cop*, to name but a few. Despite
the radical changes brought about by the women's
movement in the past several decades, women in contemporary film are seldom portrayed as principal characters around whom enthralling events unfold, although
Aliens and *Thelma and Louise* are conspicuous excep-
tions. Rarely is the heroic quest motif used to explore

the contours and dimensions of a woman's life. In his popular public television series, "The Power of Myth," the noted mythologist Joseph Campbell praised the Star Wars film series as the most compelling and inspiring contemporary enactment of the heroic tale. But as I listened to his words I wondered how he could perceive the Star Wars films as an exemplary metaphor for women when the only active characters were male. The sole female, Princess Leia, seemed to devolve over the course of events, finally becoming a scantily clad heroine who inspired Han Solo and Luke Skywalker to greater depths of spiritual and personal prowess but never developed her own. As film critic Rhoda Nottridge has observed:

> There are few heroines who have been central characters in adventure films. . . . [T]he heroine is often an observer of the action rather than a part of it. As an observer, she often appears in the role of photographer or journalist, for example, the characters of Lois Lane in the Superman films and April O'Neal in *Teenage Mutant Ninja Turtles* (1990). This gives her a career and independence, which she may not have had in earlier films. However, she still tends to be rather on the sidelines of the action.[9]

And while women and girls can derive strength and inspiration from stories of heroic men, the dearth of similar stories about women leaves many of us believing that should we strive for adventure and self-awareness, we have no alternative but to model ourselves after—or be rescued by—men.

This extant ethos affects our lives today in very harmful ways. From the religious myths of the ancient world to the secular myths of the modern world, the stereotype of the heroine reinforces the restrictive attitudes toward women in patriarchal cultures. The power of this myth makes it extremely difficult for women to be seen as strong, resourceful, courageous, and real, the ingredients of true heroic stature. Further, it has led too many women to repress or deny any desire they might feel for heroic adventure, either because they are taught to fear reprisal or because they are kept ignorant of their powerful potential.

In addition, the image of the heroine has a particularly toxic effect upon women of color. Although all women are bombarded with stories about "passive and pretty" heroines from their earliest childhood, these mass-marketed models are usually white. African-American psychologists Julia Boyd[10] and Beverly Greene,[11] Chinese-American writers Siew Hwa Beh and Judy Yung,[12] and Native American scholar Rayna Green[13] have all decried the paucity of popular stories about heroic women of color with whom younger women can identify. And Rhoda Nottridge argues that things haven't changed much in the film industry, despite the civil rights and women's movements of the past thirty years: ". . . [V]ery few films . . . have non-white central heroes,"[14] she observes, and those that do are usually male.

As I researched the history of the heroine it became painfully clear to me that women have had little hand in creating our own heroic myths. Indeed, as Sarah Pomeroy has shown, "[t]he mythology about women is created by men and, in a culture dominated by men, it may have little to do with flesh-and-blood women."[15] And it became equally clear that we will be enclosed by the boundaries of this mythology's limited vision until we begin to create our own.

I am convinced that women need a new hero myth, a new way of thinking about who we really are, what we can become, and the tasks we confront in a world overwhelmed with escalating social, political, and environmental crises. I am convinced we need a female hero myth that teaches us to claim, not suppress, the power of our femininity and to perceive ourselves as the heroes of our own lives and the authors of our own stories. I am convinced we need a hero myth that inspires us, as Carolyn Heilbrun suggests, "to take risks, to make noise, to be courageous, to become unpopular."[16] It is my hope that this book will bring this myth to birth.

CHAPTER ONE

The Journey Begins

When I was very small and learned to read, I discovered the treasures of the public library, spending hours sitting on a tiny chair, absorbed in whatever story caught my imagination. It was my greatest solace, the greatest source of adventure for my questing imagination. At the age of six I entered the realm of mythology for the first time and rapidly immersed myself in the legends of Greek, Roman, Norse, and Celtic civilizations. Although this love affair has persisted throughout my life, I knew, even as a young girl, that something was dreadfully amiss with the stories I was reading. Here were adventurous tales of boys and men who became heroes by undertaking daunting missions, solving conundrums, vanquishing evil creatures, and cavorting with magical beings. But where were the female heroes with whom *I* could identify? Occasionally a woman or girl would appear on a quest and take on a great challenge, but more often than not, she had to disguise herself as a male in order to accomplish a great deed and was retired from adventuring when her gender was discovered, usually to marriage, occasionally to martyrdom.

I had little interest in emulating the heroines I encountered in most myths and legends because, in contrast to the heroes, their lives seemed boring. Heroines were unusually beautiful and good women who sent brave men off to perform thrilling deeds and then waited to be reclaimed when the men had proven their worth. Although the myth of romantic love was something to which I aspired along with most of my peers, I wanted more. I wanted to travel to distant shores, discover the secrets of the natural and supernatural worlds, harness great creative energies, and engage in thrilling deeds. These were huge ambitions for a growing girl, ambitions for which I was often criticized, called "tomboy," and told I would outgrow when I settled down to marriage and motherhood. Fortunately I ignored most of this criticism and was rewarded with moments of high adventure and unexpected growth. But there was also a great price to pay for challenging the mold in which most females have been cast. At the age of nineteen, when my quest began in earnest, I had not anticipated that the cost of seeking to live authentically could or would be so high. I still believed that life changes were accompanied by relatively easy, smooth transitions—that a "burning bush" would appear to illuminate the new path, and that once the path was chosen, the journey would unfold pleasantly and with minimal turmoil. Although I did not know it at the time, this belief would soon be shattered, broken by the demands of a heroic quest I had not even known I was embarked upon.

Midway through my sophomore year in college I faced one of the more difficult decisions of my life. I had been raised in a family of Celtic ancestry that appeared privileged and intact to the outside world, but that was in fact a place of excruciating tension and pain. My parents were rigid and authoritarian, and my mother was full of rage and psychologically abusive toward all of their children. One child ran away several times during her early adolescence, two others suffered from severe stress-related childhood ailments, and I, at the age of fourteen, had been threatened with commitment to a juvenile detention facility for speaking out against the family's dysfunction. When this attempt failed, my mother, a deeply disturbed woman who brooked no independence from any of her children, subjected me to a year of silence and censure for refusing to conform. Meanwhile, my father retreated into work and passivity, effectively removing himself as a protective presence in any of our lives.

As a teenager, I learned to cope by throwing myself into school activities and studies, and after graduation I was able to attend college far away. But once there, my internal world began to collapse. While most of my peers were struggling with decisions about majors, professions, and boyfriends, I found myself teetering on the brink of a terrible emotional abyss with no idea where to turn for help. The college had recently contracted with a mental health organization in the city; I made an appointment to speak with a psychologist. Unfortunately, I could barely articulate the emotional horror I had experienced for so many years, and the psychologist did little to help.

I vividly remember a frigid New England morning when I walked between college buildings and suddenly knew, beyond a shadow of a doubt, that I was in imminent danger of losing myself, and that I would have to separate from my parents if I were ever to get well. But I also knew that if I did that, I would incur their wrath, rejection, and estrangement. Returning to my dormitory room in a state of shock, stricken and shaking, I sat on my bed and knew that I had to act. If I chose to remain in my family constellation, I risked losing my sanity, my hopes and dreams, perhaps even my life. But if I left, I would lose my relationship with my parents, their financial support, and the entire life and life-style I had known until then. I had no idea how to live independently, few job skills, and no resources other than those I carried within. What could and should I do? The fear and anxiety were overwhelming, but the certain knowledge that I had to act quickly overpowered those feelings. I decided to leave school, flee my home, and seek my health wherever I would find it. Without understanding the enormity of my quest, the journey had begun. . . .

In the fourteenth-century story of "Gawain and Lady Ragnell," Sir Gawain undertakes a quest to save the life of his sovereign, King Arthur, which requires him to correctly answer the question "What is it that women most desire, above all else?" Gawain meets Lady Ragnell, a powerful magician, from whom he learns that "what a woman desires above all else is the power of sovereignty, the right to exercise her own will."[1] My life experiences and those of the many remarkable women I have been privileged to know have taught me that the desire to exercise her own will and to be her most authentic self is at the heart of every woman's heroic quest. And I have also come to learn that all such quests are full of risk and uncertainty—the path to the Grail leading through deep ravines of the soul, along unmarked trails as narrow and precipitous as goat tracks in high mountain passes, through wild and unpredictable emotional weather—all to attain a vista that could be arrived at no other way.

The Grail is never achieved without trial and error, so every quester needs maps and stories to help her find her way. Myths have long been a rich and powerful source of trail guidance, for they are "clues to our deepest spiritual potential, able to lead to delight, illumination, even rapture."[2] They give us perspective, teach us about the depths and furthest reaches of our being, and show us how to journey through life consciously—that is, in resolute self-discovery.

In recent years a number of scholars have probed the old myths for new insights into women's lives. Mer-

lin Stone,[3] for example, excavated a wealth of archaeo-
logical and historical evidence about the great goddesses
who predated Judaic, Islamic, and Christian concepts of
God and documented their beneficial influence upon
women's secular and spiritual lives. Jungian analysts
Jean Shinoda Bolen,[4] Clarissa Pinkola Estes,[5] and
Andree Nicola McLaughlin examined archetypes and
legends of goddesses and wild women and created powerful new women-centered psychologies. Elaine Pagels[6]
and Fatima Mernissi[7] explored the evolution of misogynistic Christian and Islamic myths about women and
the ways they continue to contaminate our reality. Seen
as a whole, these investigations provide powerful evidence that a new mythology about women is in the
making. But as compelling as these thinkers and their
works are, they do not give mortal women sufficient
guidance for leading sovereign and authentic lives in the
temporal world.

To provide such guidance for mortal men, poets
created the myth of the hero many centuries ago. Few
other ideals have gripped the human imagination with
as much force or endured with as much affection in the
intervening years. The word *hero* is thought to have
originated in ancient Greece, where it described "one
dedicated to the great goddess Hera, the Queen of
Souls,"[8] who performed extraordinary deeds and was
recognized as an exemplary human being. Joseph
Campbell, the celebrated mythologist whose scholarly
works infused new life into this ancient subject, documented the universality of the heroic ideal and the value

of the "hero's journey"[9] for those who wish to realize their own heroic potential. Women, however, were not included among his thousand faces of the hero, because Campbell believed that "(w)oman . . . in the picture language of mythology, represents the totality of that which can be known. The hero is the one who comes to know."[10] As the following anecdote reveals, Campbell neither understood nor appreciated how many women yearn to be protagonists in heroic adventures.

> At the end of a lecture on the Arthurian quest legends about the Holy Grail, one of [Campbell's] students asked why there were no roles in the legends with which women could identify. [Campbell] was puzzled and pointed out that women are present as the hero's mother, the hero's queen, and the damsel-in-distress. "What more do you want?" he asked. "I want to be the hero, of course!" the student replied. [Campbell] was quite taken aback and muttered that he was "glad to be retiring."[11]

If the male hero has "a thousand faces," as Campbell claimed, the female hero has virtually none. This is not because heroic women are scarce or nonexistent. To the contrary. The explosion of books in recent years in such diverse fields as history, business, literature, and science reveals women's courage, ingenuity, and heroism throughout the centuries, and their many contributions to the creation of our world.[12]

For example, women have long championed the quest for equality with men. Sappho of Lesbos, a highly respected poet in the seventh century B.C., was the first in recorded history to write of women as complete human beings. Continuing in the same pro-female tradition, Mary Wollestonecraft composed *The Vindication of the Rights of Women* in the eighteenth century, the first political work that argued for women's equality. Karen Horney, the only female medical student at the University of Freiburg, Germany, in 1906, became the first psychoanalyst to refute Sigmund Freud's theories about women's development, arguing that "men's envy of women's ability to give birth was at least as important as women's supposed envy of men's penises."[13]

Perhaps nowhere, however, have women been more prominent than in the many quests for peace and social justice throughout the world. Elizabeth Fry, for instance, an eighteenth-century Quaker minister, began the prison reform movement in England when she discovered the appalling conditions in which women and their children were kept. Harriet Tubman, who escaped from slavery in 1843 and then rescued her family and more than three hundred slaves, was a leader in the abolition movement. Mercedes Comaposada founded the Mujeres Libres in Spain in 1936 to fight for women's rights and to build a community committed to the education and well-being of all people.

Women in our own time have also fought for social justice. Nawal el-Saadawi, an Egyptian feminist, physician, and writer, spent many years in prison for her books about the struggles of women in Islamic countries to achieve dignity, equality, and freedom. Australian Helen Caldicott left a thriving medical practice to found Physicians for Social Responsibility, an international organization that awakened the global population to the medical and environmental consequences of nuclear war. Another woman, Rigoberta Menchu, a Guatemalan peasant and 1992 Nobel Peace Prize recipient, learned Spanish in order to break the linguistic isolation of her people—the Quiche Indians—and told the first full story of their five-hundred-year oppression.

Women have also been at the forefront of movements for universal suffrage, education, health care, and reproductive control. Susan B. Anthony and Elizabeth Cady Stanton led the drive for women's voting rights in nineteenth-century America. At about the same time, Maria Stewart and Sarah Douglass were creating the first African-American colleges and schools, and Emily Davies was training young women to pass British university entrance examinations, an effort that led to the creation of the first women's colleges at Cambridge University. Meanwhile, Zhang Zhujun, a physician in China, was establishing hospitals and schools, fighting to end the centuries-old practice of binding women's feet, and advocating the universal education of women.

Seventeenth-century European midwives Justina Dietrich and Jane Sharp wrote two of the earliest and most comprehensive texts on childbirth and women's gynecological health, books that were widely used to train male physicians even though women had long been denied entry to the medical profession. Two hundred years later, Elizabeth Blackwell, Sophia Jex-Blake, and Elizabeth Garrett Anderson regained women's right to become physicians despite widespread and often violent opposition from male doctors and medical students. Aletta Jacobs was the first female medical doctor in the Netherlands and the first, in 1882, to establish a birth control clinic in Holland despite universal hostility and resistance. Reproductive freedom was further defended in the twentieth century by Margaret Sanger of the United States, Alexandra Kollontai of Russia, Helene Stocker of Germany, Dora Russell and Marie Stopes of England, and the millions of women throughout the world who have fought for the right to control their own bodies.

The names and deeds of heroic women could continue for thousands of pages, but that is not the point of this book. Rather, these examples attest to the fact that from the beginning of recorded history a great many women—in their own ways and in their own times—engaged with life in the time-honored tradition of the hero. These women were not isolated "geniuses," though some were more capable than others. Rather, they were ordinary women who brought about extraordinary changes in the status quo in strikingly similar ways.

First, each woman had to respond to a call to awaken, a call that asked her to live her life differently, to reconstruct the architecture of her self in some significant way, and to accomplish a greater goal than she previously could have envisioned. Each had to embark upon her quest without knowing where it would lead, and each had to evoke and depend upon depths, resources, and strengths within herself, the existence of which she may never have suspected until she answered her call. Unlike fledgling male heroes, however, most women had no female role models or allies to guide their efforts; for thousands of years the only standard of independence and achievement was male.

Second, while all heroes must undertake their quests in the absence of any guarantee of safety, security, acceptance, or survival, women had to face challenges that were wholly unique to their gender. All took the extraordinary risk of rejecting tradition and displeasing others, often jeopardizing their economic security, social status, and physical or emotional well-being, and exposing themselves to the derision and denunciation that all too often accompanied their efforts. Most were very lonely and isolated, often warned that no man would marry them, and frequently estranged from family and friends who were frightened by or hostile to women's independence.

Many were persecuted for rebelling against traditions that denied the equality of women. Hypatia of Alexandria, a fifth-century B.C. mathematician, philosopher, astronomer, and inventor, was pulled from her chariot and killed by a mob at the instigation of the patriarch of Alexandria. After transforming herself from an illiterate peasant girl to an accomplished warrior and military hero, Joan of Arc was abandoned and betrayed by those whom she had served, charged with seventy offenses (including witchcraft, heresy, and wearing and refusing to abandon male clothing), excommunicated, and executed in 1433. Annie Besant lost custody of her only daughter for advocating contraception in nineteenth-century England, and her compatriot, Emmeline Pankhurst, was jailed and released twelve times for advocating women's suffrage. Qui Jin, a poet, equestrian, swordswoman, and member of the revolutionary Chinese organization Tongmenghui, was arrested and executed in 1907 at the age of thirty-one for promoting the education of women and urging rebellion against governmental corruption and Western occupation. Even in our own time the choice to live heroically is not without its cost. As Jean Baker Miller observed,

> [A] woman's direct action can result in a combination of economic hardship, social ostracism, and psychological isolation—and even the diagnosis of a personality disorder . . . [Further,] if women assume that their own needs have equal validity and proceed to explore and state them more openly, they will be seen as creating conflict and must bear the psychological burden of rejecting men's images of "true womanhood."[14]

Third, each woman had to reject and refuse to surrender to misogynistic cultural attitudes, often internalized, that were antithetical to her quest. Each had to challenge ubiquitous beliefs that women who wanted a career or a life other than, or in addition to, children and domesticity were selfish, sexless, hostile to men and to "normal" women, and in danger of doing irreparable harm not only to their own reproductive capacity but to the future of the human species. And each had to persevere despite the knowledge that she was unlikely to achieve excellence or success on the same footing as men, no matter how skilled or talented she might be. But that was not all.

Finally, and most important, each had to envision a goal that guided her efforts and gave meaning and purpose to her life, and each had to attempt to make that dream reality, even if she failed in the process. Regardless of the nature of her particular quest, each had to believe in herself and so reach toward a greater wholeness and humanity than had ever been possible before.

How do the lives of these women illuminate the challenges we each must face if we wish to further the work they began? For answers to that question we must turn to the present.

THE PURSUIT OF OUR GREAT POSSIBILITIES

Since 1984 I have been studying giftedness in women[15]. Although "giftedness" is an emotionally laden and largely misunderstood concept, it implies the demonstration of, or potential for, exceptional ability in one or more of the following areas: intelligence, creativity, intuitive or emotional awareness, athletic prowess, and the capacity for leadership.[16] Carolyn Heilbrun captured my imagination in a vivid and fresh way when she suggested that giftedness refers not only to talent but to "a sense of great possibilities, great desires beyond the apparent possibility of fulfillment."[17] It is the pursuit of those possibilities, I believe, that defines and shapes women's heroic quests.

Over the past several years my work has brought me in contact with a large number of extraordinary women, some of whom I interviewed for this book. These women represent a wide range of ages, races, religions, and socioeconomic backgrounds and a wide variety of interests, occupations, and professions. Some are students, clients, colleagues, or friends. Some are leaders in their professions, workplaces, or communities, or advocates of social, economic, or environmental justice. Some are writers, artists, scientists, or musicians, while others are homemakers, bus drivers, gardeners, or secretaries. Some are breaking the chains of familial, cultural, and institutional dysfunction or helping others to do the same. Many are raising children, often alone, while aspiring to career goals in or outside their homes. All are pursuing their great desires and possibilities even if their chances of succeeding are small.

Like fledgling female heroes everywhere, most did not know they were embarking upon heroic quests when they began. And most had to do so in the face of enormous obstacles—lack of money; familial discouragement, opposition, and/or dysfunction; little academic or professional encouragement; inadequate preparation for independent living; limited opportunities for expressing the range of their abilities; professional isolation, particularly in nontraditional occupations; and the double bind of multiple marginality for women of color, women with disabilities, and lesbians. Many were punished at some time in their lives for displaying talents and skills unexpected or undesired in women. Many expressed a long-standing distrust of their femininity because throughout their lives it was used to repress or constrain the development of their potential. Many have no female mentors or role models to inspire them and affirm their aspirations, leaving them with a strong sense of psychological wariness and spiritual loneliness.

Despite these obstacles, these women display an extraordinary degree of courage, integrity, and commitment to their goals. They are also passionate, enthusiastic, and psychologically complex, and they remain open to life even in the face of adversity and pain. But like their historical sisters, most do not think their efforts to live authentic and sovereign lives are heroic in nature, and they are uncomfortable when the word *hero* is applied to them (a feeling with which readers are likely to identify). Part of their discomfort stems from the fact that the concept of the hero has traditionally implied elitism, singularity, and separation from the community, values that many women immediately reject. But as I will argue throughout this book, this need not be the case. Part of the discomfort derives from women's igno-

rance of our own heroic history. Because the stories of
female heroes are rarely told, women seldom perceive
their own lives as heroic journeys. Few of us realize that
heroes are not born fully formed, nor are they superhu-
man; rather, they are fully *human* beings who are forged
in the crucible of change, a process fraught with uncertainty, pain, and despair, and demanding heroic responses to life events. I have heard many women
disclaim the heroism of their lives, believing that struggling with difficult life experiences disqualifies them as
female heroes, and I suspect some readers will feel the
same. But these are the very experiences that can transform a woman into a hero if she can see her life from
that perspective.

I have written this book for two reasons. First, I,
like Joseph Campbell, think the hero is a universal ideal
that helps people think about their lives in a more profound and creative way, and I believe that women will
gain a greater sense of self if we see the challenges of our
lives from the empowering perspective of the hero-path.
Second, I hope to create a model of psychological and
spiritual resilience, resistance to the status quo, and responsibility to the larger community of which we are
members. Psychologists such as Carol Gilligan[18] and
Emily Hancock[19] have written powerfully about wom-
en's robust, spirited, pre-adolescent selves who all but
disappear when we reach adolescence. How do we keep
those selves alive and bring them to adulthood with our
spirits intact? How do we live sovereign and authentic
lives not only for our own sakes but for the sake of each

other and our world? My response to these questions will be found in this book.

In the following pages I will use the terms *quester* and *female hero* to encourage readers to change the way they think about their lives. *The Sound of a Silver Horn* will explore the classical heroic quest through the lives of contemporary women. It will look for answers to four questions suggested by the male hero's journey, which is said to occur in three stages: a call to adventure or self-awareness, a decision to embark upon this mysterious journey and face whatever challenges arise, and, finally, a transformation to a more profound sense of self and involvement with the larger world. What is the female hero's journey? Where do the male and female quests converge and diverge? What new model of female heroism can emerge to replace the image of the heroine, which is no longer viable? And how can we use this model to restore and reshape our personal, community, and planetary lives?

Stories from the lives of many women, including my own, are told in the following pages. To gather these stories I developed and sent to 150 women an open-ended questionnaire that asked them to reflect upon their life experiences from the perspective of the heroic quest. Thirty-five women chose to respond, and many of their stories are woven into the fabric of these pages. Seven agreed to participate in an extensive and structured interview that elaborated on their written responses. All their names have been altered or omitted to protect their privacy.

If this book has one central message to convey, it is that heroism is not something "out there," attainable by only one woman in every thousand or million. The heroic quest is a journey upon which every woman is embarked wherever she is in her life at whatever moment, even though she may not recognize her life as such. It is my hope that the experiences of the women whose lives comprise this book will encourage readers to reevaluate their concepts of heroism, rethink where true heroism lies, place themselves at various stages along the heroic journey, and thereby see more clearly the way ahead. By drawing upon the optimism and dynamism of the myth of the heroic quest, by seeing how other contemporary women are cultivating their heroic potential, every woman can transform her own life and empower those around her to do the same.

When Joseph Campbell called contemporary men to the hero's journey, he observed that to undertake this quest without a guide would be a hopeless endeavor. Fortunately, he argued, ". . . we have not even to risk the adventure alone; for the heroes of all time have gone before us; the labyrinth is thoroughly known; we have only to follow the thread of the hero-path."[20] Unlike the men for whom this hero-path was so painstakingly composed, women have had to risk the adventure alone, for the female hero-path has not been drawn before. And so now, as we turn to her, we must use our minds, our hearts, and our collective midwifery to bring her to birth, and follow her quest for wholeness through the labyrinth of our own lives. I asked each of the women I interviewed or queried to help me envision the female hero and chart her hero-path. What follows is a portrait drawn from these perceptions. It is only a map, only a beginning. But it is a start.

CHAPTER TWO

The Call to Awaken

W hen I fled my parents' home to reclaim my emotional health, I plunged into a life for which I was totally unprepared. Four months after that first, startling call to awaken, I withdrew from college, borrowed $100 from a friend, and set up housekeeping with three other women in a tiny, cockroach-infested apartment in Boston. Although I had no idea how to live independently or build a new life, necessity was truly my mother of invention. During my first year of emancipation I held a series of low-paying, mind-numbing jobs, none of which I kept for very long, for each reminded me all too painfully of how much had changed in my life. My mother's response to my bid for independence was as severe as I had feared it might be; she forbade me entry to her home and severed our relationship, actions to which my father acquiesced. I could not fathom the malevolence behind their actions, and though it confirmed in me my decision to escape, the pain was often unbearable. In response I threw myself into antiwar and women's rights activities and spent several months writing letters and speeches for an African-American mayoral candidate, experiences that gave my life a much-needed sense of meaning and purpose.

At the conclusion of this political campaign I joined the corps of VISTA volunteers, working with a group of dedicated social activists to provide consumer protection and legal-aid services for the poor of Boston. But as this second year waned, so did my spirits. The continuing estrangement from my parents left me deeply depressed, and there were grim days when I wondered how I would ever survive. Yet I was unwilling to give up without a fight; somehow, I believed, even this experience must have a purpose—if only I could figure out what it was.

As the end of my commitment to VISTA approached I was paralyzed with uncertainty about what to do next. I had to find another job, but I could not motivate myself to look for work because Boston felt like the wrong place to be. But where else could I go? One evening in early June I had an extraordinary dream in which a being appeared and counseled me to leave the East Coast and "go west." "You're crazy," my dream self said, a verdict with which my waking self wholeheartedly concurred. I proceeded to ignore the dream's advice, ruminating instead over various possibilities for employment. Little did I know the ways of the unconscious at that point in my life. The dream repeated itself over the next few weeks, becoming more insistent with each recurrence. Finally I awoke in the middle of one such dream and cried in frustration, "Okay, I'll go, now let me get some sleep!" The dream guide smiled, a bit smugly I thought, and wafted away like wisps of smoke.

Well, now what? I wondered. I had no money, no car, no idea of where or what "the west" was, and no one to stay with if I could manage to get there. Yet I knew nothing remained for me in Boston but more uncertainty and despair, neither of which I could endure for much longer. So like the Fool in the tarot, I decided to trust this curious dream and stride into the unknown. When my VISTA contract expired in September I collected my small severance allowance, gave away my few possessions, loaded up my backpack, and set off in search of a new way of life.

The heroic quest begins when a call to adventure or self-awareness asks us to leave behind our personal past and embark upon a journey that will change our lives forever. In conventional myths and fairy tales heroines are aroused from the slumber of their lives by falling in love, and some fledgling heroes may be similarly awakened. But most are called to their quests in other ways.

Joan, a nun and highly placed administrator in the Roman Catholic Church, remembered an awakening that occurred more than fifty years ago. "I came out of a European and Protestant background," she confided. "My family was Mormon, and I was the youngest of three children, the only daughter. And as a very young child I knew that there was some seed of vision, something that was stretching me to be other than Mormon. I lived in a neighborhood with Catholic children; they were my friends and we always played together, and sometimes I would attend church with them, unbeknownst to my parents. I was mystified and attracted, somewhat spellbound by the ritual in the Catholic Church, and in the fourth grade I wrote a letter to the pastor of the parish asking him if I could come into that church. Unfortunately he wrote a letter to my parents, after which they said there would be no further contact with that church. But my father and I were close friends; we'd do things together on Saturday mornings. I remember going to his office with him and watching black-garbed sisters walking through the snow, and I said one day I will be one of them."

Joan's mother died when Joan was nine, and on her deathbed she wrote a letter giving her daughter permission to enter the Catholic Church if she still wished to do so. A few years later her father remarried, and Joan's new stepmother—also her eighth-grade teacher—encouraged her to attend a Catholic girls' high school. This, she said, was a turning point because it enabled her to develop her intellect in a challenging environment without having to compete with boys or downplay her abilities. Upon graduation her stepmother urged her to attend college, but Joan's childhood awakening was reasserting its strong pull. Instead of following her stepmother's advice she decided to enter a religious community, accepting "the compulsion to be part of this life-style that was so completely different from any other career that young women would choose at that time." So began an adventure that would lead her down paths she could never have foreseen.

A quester may awaken through a dream or an intuition, an accident or a chance encounter, or a part of herself that yearns to be expressed. Kristen grew up in a close and loving interracial family; her mother is black and her father is white, and they and her three sisters "are all extremely successful in conventional ways." But she wanted to work in public health, preventing unwanted pregnancies and sexually transmitted diseases. "I always knew my profession would involve some sort of controversial issue and not be well compensated financially," Kristen said. "Although I think my family has always felt some pride in me, there was always family pressure to conform, to be different from who I wanted to be. So as I was finishing school I realized that I could not move back to the same city and create the kind of life I wanted, because the choices I wanted to make conflicted with my upbringing and my family's values. The biggest change in my life came when I saw that I had to be away from them in order to do the things I felt were most myself. It was a more powerful awareness than any I had previously experienced, and it's one that I continue to struggle with. Even though I'm close to my family and have love and affection for them, I am unable to handle the kind of pressure they put on me to be more like them."

Some awakenings begin in relative calm, born from an image of what we might become, but others slam into our lives with gale force, wresting us from the grip of personal, cultural, or familial patterns the extent of which we may not suspect until the journey is well advanced. Occasionally the breakdown of a woman's health forces her to reassess the contours of the life she has been living. Ariel was sitting at the kitchen table drinking orange juice in the early-morning sunlight when a blood vessel burst in her brain and she suffered a stroke. She was twenty-nine years old. "You know," she said, many months after her recovery began, "I always knew on some deep level that it would take a serious physical problem to enable me to detach from my family's crippling expectations and figure out who I really was and what I wanted to do with my life. So in a way when the stroke happened, I wasn't surprised. It was a shock, but somehow I knew exactly what was happening and why, and that if I chose to live I would have to live on my own terms rather than theirs."

No one undertakes the challenge of awakening with ease, even those to whom change comes without great resistance. No matter what form her call takes and no matter how much she needs to leave her old life behind, the fledgling hero is always reluctant to respond. And so painful or traumatic experiences often conspire to foist the heroic life upon her: a relationship disappoints or disappears; a job is lost or fails to materialize; someone or something or some important part of herself is lost and she becomes frightened, confused, and depressed. These events may seem random and chaotic at first, but they are neither. Rather, their purpose is to compel the quester to relinquish her familiar but ill-fitting life and discover new depths, resources, and possibilities within herself and take responsibility for consciously creating her life anew, for becoming a more fully functioning human being. And whether a quest is born from crisis, enthusiasm, blunder, or conscious resolution, "the adventure that the hero is ready for is the one [she] gets."[1]

"This is a story I've told only to two people, my husband and you," said Zena, sitting in her study with a faraway expression in her dark Middle Eastern eyes. Zena was born in Lebanon some years before civil war erupted there, the eldest child of five, surrounded by a large extended family. At the time we spoke she had been in this country for nine years, had just achieved citizenship, and was managing a research project for a health care organization. "I was seven or eight years old, going to Catholic school, and I was in the kitchen with my mother. We were talking about some bugs that came in a jar of rice and I was questioning: If God had created everything, did He create the bugs? And how did the bugs come to be in the jar? And asking questions about religion and God. And then all of a sudden there was a slap on my face, and my mother saying that I shouldn't be asking those kinds of questions. And this, I think, was my first moment of awareness. I knew I was living in a place surrounded by people telling me what I should believe, what I should ask, what I should think, but I decided after this experience not to believe anything anymore. I resolved to ask about everything."

What made this decision especially difficult, Zena said, was that in Lebanon values and beliefs about religion and behavior were fixed and forced upon people. "All kids, not only girls, were required to behave according to certain rules: obey without questioning, don't answer back to your parents, don't argue, be polite, kiss your grandmother, all kinds of things that are probably meaningless to adults. But that was our world, and it was imposed on us. So I started this questioning when I was eight, and by the time I reached twelve I didn't want to have anything to do with the status quo. I didn't want to be a young girl the way young girls were supposed to be. By the time I was thirteen I wanted to do political work, which not many young girls did, so I started that. But at the beginning I was alone. I didn't have anybody to guide me."

Zena remained politically active throughout her adolescence, much to the chagrin of her immediate community. Then, at age eighteen, she entered Beirut University, attending as consistently as the war permitted. The university would close for a year because of the fighting, then reopen, but Zena was able to complete her bachelor's degree in biology and master's degree in biology education, a field she had chosen because "this was an avenue that was more open to me than any other at that time, and I was encouraged to go into it. I didn't want to be a physician because I'm afraid of shots," she laughed. "I didn't want to be an engineer. I wanted to be an airline pilot, but this was a huge dream for a little girl then. I wanted flying, probably because I lived near the airport as a child and I was fascinated with planes. Maybe because I wanted to be free of a place that's narrow in a physical sense, narrow in an abstract sense, narrow from every which way you take it. Flying was a powerful symbol for me. I still have this feeling that is hard to describe when the plane takes off. There is nothing that can compare with that moment; it's one of my favorite times. Flying was a dream and a passion, but there was no way I could do it. There was no precedent and nobody to help me live that dream. There wasn't even an institute that would take girls who wanted to be airline pilots. And that was something that would have caused my family great pain had I found a way to do it. In one way I wanted to be different, but I love my parents so much that I really couldn't hurt them like this. So even with me as a rebel, I chose something that pleased them."

Zena was determined to rise above the chaos of civil war. Although teaching was not her passion, she became the top student in her discipline at Beirut University and won a fellowship to study science education anywhere in the world. After investigating a variety of possibilities she found herself choosing between promising programs in France and the United States, a decision influenced in no small way by language. Although fluent in Lebanese, Arabic, and French, she possessed only a smattering of English at the time, two or three phrases like "How are you?" and "Where is a restaurant?" and

"How can I find a hotel?" To undertake any level of education in a second or third language is arduous, but to pursue a doctorate in a foreign culture while learning an entirely new language seemed a formidable challenge. "Well, other people have done it," Zena said. "It doesn't mean that it wasn't scary to land, like you're landing on the moon. I only knew three people here, and this was the extent of my community. I had the choice to go to France, which would have been easier, but I decided since I was leaving I wanted something really new, a completely different experience." Her decision was made during a discussion with one of her professors at Lebanese University. "He said, 'Zena, why don't you go to France? There is a big Lebanese community there. And it will be just like home.' And as soon as he said, 'It will be just like home,' I said I'm not going there. 'You know the language. The people are close to us in their behavior, beliefs, and social structure,' he said. But I didn't want that anymore. So I decided I was going to a place very far away if I was going at all. Otherwise I'd stay home. I never had a doubt that I could do it. So I flew myself here and I did it."

No one can predict the timing of an awakening, how long it will last, or how a woman's life, relationships, and familiar self will change as a result. Sometimes a period of discontent precedes an awakening, preparing a woman for the possibility, necessity, and inevitability of change. Rikki, a twenty-two-year-old cosmetician, grew up in a family plagued by her father's alcoholism and physical violence and her mother's chronic illness. Although Rikki was very bright, neither of her parents ever encouraged her to study or take herself seriously. Consequently she spent most of her adolescence dropping in and out of high school, hanging out on the streets, and going nowhere very fast. But during her senior year she looked around and realized that if she did not take possession of her life, her adulthood would be as bleak as her childhood.

With the encouragement of a high school counselor Rikki enrolled in beauty school and learned a trade that enabled her to support herself and move away from home. But as her twenty-third birthday approached she felt increasingly restless and bored; she watched as some of her friends created more satisfying lives while others lost themselves in dysfunctional relationships, financial irresponsibility, or drug abuse. She talked about becoming a teacher but found multiple excuses for not making the commitment. One morning, in a burst of frustration, she dyed her blond hair brown, a decision she spent the rest of the day loathing. But that evening she sat down and asked herself what exactly she was trying to tell herself. She realized she had been circling around the biggest change she needed to make, altering every aspect of herself except the one that mattered most. The next day she restored her hair to its former color and resolved to get out of debt, go back to school, and create the life she most wanted to live.

Some awakenings are very abrupt, calling a woman to free herself immediately from whatever chains her to the past. But others are extremely subtle, having their genesis at an earlier point in a woman's life and coming to fruition only when growth and circumstances permit their activation.

Melia, a native of the Philippine Islands, psychosocial nurse practitioner and mother of three sons, was aware of the discrepancy between her own ideas and those of her culture from the time she was very young. Melia was a middle child in a large, loving family, a bright, inquisitive girl whose ambitions, intelligence, and ideas were threatening to an Asian culture that did not allow women the same freedom of expression granted to men. "My family was very disapproving of me," she recalled. "They were very disapproving that I was intelligent and showed it. Intelligence was great, and I was praised for mine as long as it showed only on the report card. But if I actually displayed it, that was different, because girls in my country do not speak up. It was considered disrespectful, exhibitionistic, and just completely wrong to show superiority or any kind of confidence—not only as a girl, but as a girl child. So that was a very confusing experience. They knew I was smart and disapproved of my showing it, but I showed it anyway. There's no way I could hide. It's almost like a force that comes out. I played dumb for two hours, but I couldn't stand it. I'd rather die," she laughed, "or be incapacitated or something. Asleep. That's the only docile moment in me. Otherwise they always knew I was like this."

When she was sixteen Melia entered college, enrolling in a five-year nursing program; two years later, she recalled, she was introduced to ideas that would change her life dramatically. "During the third year we were taught about psychiatric concepts and I got very excited, more excited than I had ever been before. I started putting myself in the role of psychotherapist, and I just knew that's what I would be. But when I tried to fit the role into Philippine culture I saw there was no way I would ever make a living out of it. There is no acceptance of psychotherapists in my culture. In the Philippines, family is supposed to be self-sufficient. Everybody in the family should be a psychotherapist, so to speak, everybody should be able to support and provide insight. The head 'psychotherapist' is the oldest and wisest—say a grandfather or great-grandfather or great-grandmother. People go to that person for advice and for clarity, for support, for anything that is out of the ordinary. There is an unspoken rule that you do not go outside the family. So there was no place for me there."

Melia decided to emigrate to the United States after graduation to realize her dissident dream, although she knew no one in this country and English was her third and least-fluent language. "I told no one of my plans," she said, "until I finished interviewing for jobs." She accepted a contract to work in the South as a medical-surgical nurse because after its completion she would be free to pursue her education anywhere she wished. Then she acquired a visa and an airplane ticket. "Nobody in the family knew I was going to the States because of the control the parents have on their kids. You are supposed to ask their permission for everything. But I knew that would be difficult for me, so I made sure everything was set up, and then two months before my departure I told them I would be leaving. And then they were supportive, maybe because they know me. I always did what I had to do, and they always knew that if I said I would do something, I'd do it. So I guess in that sense they had no choice."

"I'm different from my siblings in that way," Melia continued, "and I always knew it. I made decisions as a very young girl about what I would be and what kind of family I would have. And I'm not talking about intellectualizing. My vision was formulated according to how I was feeling also. I knew what kind of plan I would have, how many kids, and so on, and I just knew it would happen." She laughed at the memory of her feisty younger self, adding, "I was an adolescent then, and you know that in adolescence people think they're so powerful."

Sarah is another woman whose awakening was set in motion during her childhood, but the trauma she experienced then left her unable to answer the call until her early middle age. Sarah grew up in a white, Southern, Presbyterian family; her mother had been diagnosed as schizophrenic in the late 1940s, before psychotropic medications enabled psychiatrically disabled individuals to live successfully in the community. When Sarah was five years old and her sister three, their mother was committed to a state hospital, where she remained until she died at the age of seventy-eight. Sarah's father coped as best he could, but the strain took its toll and he started drinking, eventually becoming alcoholic. When she was nine her father remarried; Sarah experienced her stepmother as cold and aloof and was frightened of her throughout her childhood and adolescence.

For years she felt she was carrying around a terrible secret. "My mother was crazy and I couldn't tell anyone about it. I couldn't talk about my past because I felt that everybody else was 'normal' and I was not. I didn't feel safe enough with anyone to talk about this, and I felt much younger than I was chronologically, just like a little kid. Years later when I got into therapy I would regress back into earlier ages, and I realized that when I was under stress those younger selves would try to make my decisions for me. This was because as a child I always felt I had to grow myself up. My father was only there sometimes, and I was scared of my stepmother just like I was scared of my mother. I had to take care of myself, so I watched other people a lot to find out what 'normal' was and how to do it. And I made a decision early on that I could never depend on other people, that I could only depend on myself."

Sarah's call to awaken was preceded by her decision at twenty-seven, to terminate her work as a secretary and enter a professional training program in social work. This was the first time she recalls undertaking an education for herself. "When I went through college I was doing it for my family. I got married at age twenty-one because I thought it was expected of me. I felt like

I was living under the expectations of the world, not that anyone had ever said they had those expectations for me. But I started graduate school during the time of the women's movement, and I felt I was really challenging myself, learning new things, and doing things for myself for the first time."

Although this was a pivotal decision in Sarah's life, it did not register as a moment of awakening. That was to come several years after she completed her degree and embarked upon her new career. "The time I recall very vividly," she said, "was when I was thirty years old and already a social worker. Although I had finished school, I felt very insecure about my abilities, so I decided to get into a training program to learn specific techniques and styles of doing therapy. I was married at the time, and my husband, who was also a social worker, was quite confident in his skills. I met a psychiatrist and his wife who were planning to start a group practice and a training center, and my husband and I decided to get into the training part of the program. Shortly thereafter we were asked if we wanted to join their practice. I said yes, but I didn't feel that I really knew anything.

"As part of this training," she continued, "I had an opportunity to attend a weekend workshop where the psychiatrist was the trainer and my therapist for the session. One of the things I discovered that weekend was that I had buried a lot of things about my family and my past, and those things just started coming out. And I realized that if I didn't make some major changes in my life, at least acknowledge some of the skeletons in my closets, I wouldn't be able to do the type of work I had set out to do. So I entered therapy and a whole new world opened up for me. I woke up and started to face everything I had been afraid to see before."

"Awakenings are the result of suppressed desires and conflicts," Joseph Campbell wrote. "They are the ripples on the surface of life, produced by unsuspected springs."[2] But though they arise from the unconscious realms of the self, they require a woman to respond consciously, to accept the invitation to create herself anew, and to undertake the challenge no matter how frightened or inadequate she may feel. Thus, each awakening call demands not only that it be heard, but that the woman find the courage to trust and affirm the call whenever it arises, wherever it takes her, and however much it challenges her way of being in the world.

Affirming one's quest in the midst of turmoil is never easy; the difficulties can seem so overwhelming that a woman may want to give up before she begins. But the self who awakens, initiates, and transforms us has an infinite number of tricks up her sleeve, and always attempts to evoke our heroic potential. "So it is that sometimes the predicament following . . . a refusal of the call proves to be the occasion of a providential revelation of some unsuspected principle of release."[3]

Annie is a second-generation Jewish American whose ancestors came "from all over Europe." She was born into a military family that moved frequently during her childhood until the unexpected death of her mother when she was nine. From that moment, she said, "I was very aware that I was going to be a different person. We had an automobile accident and were all in the hospital, and my father came to my hospital bed and told me my mother had died. We were out of town and the whole rest of the family had driven down. He talked to me for a couple of minutes and I cried for a while, and then he said that my grandmother had collapsed and that I had to help him take care of her because she needed me. And one of the things she said to me was that I was going to have to take care of my father because he was all I had in the world and I was all he had. I was a different person from those two statements and knew it. It was a visceral feeling. I'm an only child," she added, "and I took real seriously that I had to take care of these people."

Shortly after her mother's death Annie and her father went to live with her Orthodox grandparents. "It was very clear that the expectations for me were going to become—I'm not sure whether I want to say 'greater' or 'different.' I was certainly fulfilling a dual role for my mother's parents, both as a stand-in for my mother, who was very young when she died and considered to be very capable, and as myself. I don't think my father had that set of expectations, but my grandparents did, and I was definitely aware of that. I became a very good girl and tried to do everything right and tried to know absolutely everything there was to know and was very frightened of making any kind of error that would indicate that there were lots of things I didn't know. So I faked a lot."

When Annie was thirteen her father married a woman she dearly loved, an event that gave her an enormous sense of freedom but left her without a sense of identity or direction for many years to come. "I took that as my opportunity to be a fluff and stop fulfilling anybody's expectations, including mine," Annie said. "I went through a period of years where I wasn't very good at all anymore. I stopped producing in school. I didn't talk in class. I wanted to be pretty, wanted to be popular, and had a very hard time because I couldn't quite do it. I experienced a great deal of discomfort during that period. At sixteen I went away to a large university instead of the Seven Sisters college I was supposed to attend because I thought it made more sense to follow a boy than to get an education. All the while I was being told that I was bright enough to do anything I wanted. During my first semester of college my parents had to come up and intervene because I never went to class and was about to be thrown out, but I got good grades so they were having trouble finding grounds for expelling me. That was a very rough period, which resulted in my getting married at nineteen."

Annie dropped out of college to marry and shortly thereafter left with her new husband for Africa, where he was doing graduate work in art history. "And that put me in an entirely different culture. I don't know whether it forced or enabled me to look at some things that I hadn't looked at before in terms of what my role was, what I was doing, and why I was doing it. I read a tremendous amount while we were gone. I taught and ran a school without really knowing what I was doing. But I think that was my first big growing-up period because it became clear to me rather quickly that just being married was not going to do what I had decided it was supposed to—which was be totally satisfying."

Annie and her husband came home to the States when her first child was six weeks old and returned to Africa with two children for a second year when they were two and five. "And during that trip I worked with my husband, which was good because I was able to do some research and participate in some of the things that were going on. But it was almost like the time overseas was time out of space. It was good time, and it was probably the most satisfying time in a lot of ways, but it wasn't real. It was pretend time because we had to come home, and I still didn't feel I belonged." For several years thereafter Annie was deeply depressed, unable to "settle down to what I should have been doing. You know, I joined the League of Women Voters and I did the co-op preschool and I did all those kinds of things and it just wasn't enough. It just didn't feel right." As Annie delved into the causes of her depression, she came to realize that neither marriage nor motherhood could give her the fulfillment she needed from her life; for that she must look to herself. So when her youngest child was five she signed up for a correspondence course and returned to school, taking the first step along a path that would lead to a career in gifted education.

The decision to embark upon a heroic quest is one that only the quester can make, and it is never easily made, for every woman who chooses to awaken is by that action no longer the same person. The call to the quest throws open a window into a woman's soul, offering her a glimpse of her deepest desires and her greatest possibilities. The moment of awakening never lasts for long, but if she is willing to peer through this window she will perceive the direction in which her spirit yearns to grow, and its impact on her own life will be profound and far-reaching.

Leah, the eldest child and only daughter born to midwestern parents of Russian Jewish decent, remembers her early childhood as one of great happiness, and she felt much loved by her adoring and adored parents. But when she was six years old she was suddenly and irrevocably expelled from this paradise. Leah's mother, after the birth of her youngest son, fell into a severe postpartum depression from which she never recovered. "She just sort of dropped out of sight and the family fell apart," Leah said. "She got very needy and narcissistic and my father got withdrawn and demanding. I ended up doing a lot of caretaking because they both leaned on me a lot." One aftershock of this familial earthquake was a prodigious battle with depression and food, a struggle that lasted well into Leah's early adulthood.

When she was nineteen, Leah was jolted awake by two electrifying events: her discovery of the women's movement and of her lesbianism. Suddenly, she said, "things made sense. I realized that the issues being raised by feminists were important to me. Until that time I was a very male-identified young woman. I liked men better, I hung out with them. I realize now," she laughed, "that it was in part because we had more things in common, like the object of our sexual attraction."

As an undergraduate in the early 1970s, Leah was involved in anti–Vietnam War and radical Jewish student activities; slowly she came to realize how badly women were treated in both of those movements, and during a conference of the National Radical Zionist Alliance in 1971 she suddenly woke up. "Five other people and I all drove up to Wisconsin. Eight women attended the conference, two of whom were there as girlfriends of two of the guys. The other six of us were local organizers, as were the thirty or so men in attendance. During the conference we women got together and talked about the fact that these guys were willing to pass resolutions in support of every single liberation movement in the whole world except ours. We questioned why there were so few women among the organizers and why we were treated with such disrespect, and why the men were so uncomfortable with our decision to meet on our own that they sent their girlfriends in to check out our meeting. It was not as if any of us were strongly identified with feminism in 1971, it just made intuitive sense to say, 'We want to get together by ourselves and talk about these issues.' And that was the beginning."

This awakening opened Leah to a view of life profoundly different from any she had previously seen, and when she returned home she began to write a women's column for the radical Jewish student paper. "Around that time there were some women's liberation groups happening in Cleveland, and I started attending consciousness-raising meetings. And then I fell in love with another woman and realized that this was something incredibly important that was going to change how I understood my life. It became connected to how I live my life, to the choices I make, to absolutely everything I do. And so those were the first things that made me sit up and take notice."

As Leah's words suggest, awakenings are not solitary events occurring only in the dim recesses of an individual's past. The heroic quest is a cyclic process fueled by a woman's curiosity, courage, and capacity for growth, qualities that propel her from awakening to transformation and contain within themselves the seeds of new adventures. This describes what happened to Jane, who entered a Roman Catholic religious community at the age of eighteen when she realized she wanted to live "a life of excellence rather than end up in a boring marriage and life like that of my parents." Her next awakening occurred six years later when she was preparing to take her final vows. "I realized that the vow of obedience made no sense to me anymore," she said. "I thought exercising my free will and making decisions was a superior way to live to blindly following the dictates of others. I grew to dislike the hierarchy of men in Rome and felt they were insensitive to the needs of women. I resented that women had no power in the Church." Valuing freedom and the ability to make her own decisions, Jane did not renew her vows when they expired. Instead she left her order and her church so that she could "savor the search for the meaning of life" on her own.

Eileen escaped from her painfully abusive alcoholic family at the age of seventeen by marrying and setting up what she believed to be the "perfect home." Twelve years later she awoke to a deep need to be more than an ideal wife and mother, but it was not a need her husband would support. After two years of counseling Eileen decided to leave her marriage and take her four children with her. Her husband refused to provide any child support unless she returned to him and her former role, something she could not allow herself to do. Because she had no education and could not receive adequate help from the public welfare system, she decided to move closer to her family. "Since my father, the alcoholic, was dead by now and I was naïve to our family dysfunction, I didn't see that the worst was yet to come—my mother's need for codependent relationships and my three brothers' accommodating alcoholism."

By the time she was thirty-six Eileen knew she had to leave home again, but this time she was determined to do it consciously and well. She set up housekeeping some distance away, entered group therapy, and redefined her relationships with every member of her family, terminating those that were toxic. After three of the "most serene, if lonely" years of her life, she was ready to enter another marriage, a partnership that has survived enormous stresses for more than sixteen years because of a mutual commitment to grow as individuals and as a couple.

But Eileen's awakenings were far from over. When she was forty-eight she decided to leave a job she had held for five years and become a full-time college student. "It was a particular risk since my husband had been back to work for only a year after a two-year battle with cancer," Eileen said. "During those years we had witnessed four family deaths and lost our battle to see a beloved grandchild. Somewhat bottomed out, I knew I needed something solid in my life, and we both felt that if he were to become ill again my education was our best investment. We decided to gamble our retirement funds to put me through school. Now, at fifty-two, I do have something solid: I have a wonderful community of friends and alumni, I am better prepared to work even if older, and in his fifth year of remission my husband can relax a little. This has been my most significant changing time of all."

As each of these stories suggests, awakenings spring from the depths of our being and take their shape from the hopes, dreams, and purposes from which we fashion our lives on a moment-to-moment basis. Although they can burst into consciousness with dazzling speed and throw our lives into utter disarray, they are neither arbitrary nor meaningless. Rather, they are clear indications of the authentic self seeking to take form. Yet what transmutes a seemingly capricious event into an awakening is the quester herself, for she must choose to perceive herself as someone who is invited to set forth upon a remarkable journey of growth and transformation, and not as a victim of circumstances beyond her control.

Unfortunately some women forgo that journey because it is fraught with danger and undertaken at great cost—sometimes to our relationships with parents or partners, sometimes to our friendships and sense of community or belonging, and sometimes to our emotional and physical well-being. Although answering the call to awaken may seem, at times, an impossible feat, the alternative is intellectually, emotionally and spiritually lethal. If a woman refuses to answer the call she will never arrive at the threshold of transformation and discover what she is truly capable of being. Instead she will live in constant fear of what she will not see, a feeling that only grows stronger with time, eclipsing her spirit and leaving a thick sludge of emptiness, rage, and bitterness in its wake. An awakening is a gift that can always be refused, but at far greater cost than a woman may suspect, for the more a woman clings to sleep, the more circumscribed and stagnant her life will become. As a passage in an ancient Nag Hammadi text warns, "If you bring forth what is within you, what you bring forth will save you. If you do not bring forth what is within you, what you do not bring forth will destroy you."[4]

Unlike those classical heroines who lay suspended in sleep until a prince aroused them from their spell, the female hero must wake herself up. To do this she must draw upon her inmost reserves of strength, courage, hope, and resolve. No fledgling hero knows where her journey will lead or what will be required of her along the way. No one undertakes a quest without feeling alone, uncertain, frightened, and confused. The call to

awaken does not guarantee happiness, health, or the sur-
cease of suffering, but it does promise great adventure.
It invites us to explore the depths of ourselves and to
risk becoming what is in each of us to be. And if a
woman accepts this call, she is projected forthwith onto
the path of initiation.

CHAPTER THREE

The Dragons of Initiation

*I*s any stage of the journey more difficult and demanding than the others? If there is, it is surely the initiation, because the quester often believes that having answered the call to awaken, her life will automatically become better. Not so. The experiences of the initiation are catalysts that dissolve or transmute the hero's personal past and enable her to live out the potential only hinted at during her awakening.

The initiation is the time Christian mystics call the "dark night of the soul," the time described by Native Americans as the "vision quest." It is a period of profound change, challenge, and tribulation. As Carol Pearson and Katherine Pope maintain, "the budding hero has all the capacities she needs, but they are latent."[1] Thus, the purpose of the initiation is to release these capacities and hidden strengths by presenting a series of formidable obstacles. These obstacles or "dragons" invariably seem insurmountable, but they must be overcome if the quester is to realize her authentic potential. The challenges of the initiation will break the hold of her personal past, shatter whatever chains bind her to an outworn image of herself, and free her for her transformation.

THE FIRST DRAGON

After leaving her familiar world the quester enters a period characterized by ordeal, chaos, emptiness, and often despair. The first and most formidable dragon she must confront is her own self, a task poignantly described by the Sufi poet Omar Khayyám in his *Rubáiyát*: "I sent my Soul through the Invisible / Some Letter of that After-Life to spell / And by and by my Soul return'd to me / And answer'd 'I myself am Heav'n and Hell.' "[2]

One of my most memorable encounters with this dragon occurred many years ago in the form of a harrowing nightmare. I found myself standing on a hilltop surrounded by three small children, battling a dark and ferocious storm that filled the sky as far as I could see. After an interminable and exhausting battle the darkness receded, gradually moving to the limit of the horizon and finally disappearing. The four of us were jubilant, and we began to dance and sing about our victory, but suddenly a child looked up and screamed. As I followed her pointing finger I saw that the darkness had gathered itself and was returning; feeling frightened and discouraged, I knew I had little strength left with which to fight. Suddenly a voice interrupted my fear, telling me that only if I had the courage to view the face of that darkness would it ever truly disappear. With great trepidation I agreed and was immediately brought into a dark room and placed in a protective pool of water. A door set into a recessed corner opened and a figure, cloaked in a high-collared black robe, emerged, slowly progressing along the length of the room. Suddenly it turned toward me, its face illuminated with an eerie light, and I found myself staring into my own eyes. I awoke screaming in terror and could not regain sleep for hours thereafter. The dream was so powerful and so disturbing that I set about the very next day to understand what I had seen in myself.

Two months after I left the East Coast in search of a new home, a journey described in more detail in chapter 4, I found what I was looking for in Seattle, a city I loved at first sight. Although the initial adjustment was far more difficult than I had expected it to be, within the year things settled into place. I started a new relationship, found a secretarial job with an innovative juvenile-justice project, and returned to college to continue my education.

The next few years were pivotal, punctuated by the search for a meaningful use of my abilities and meaningful relationships with kindred spirits. I completed a bachelor's degree in prelaw and a master's degree in counseling and after a time found paid work in my chosen but overpopulated field. Yet despite these achievements I felt a deep and underlying turmoil, which no accomplishment could quell. Until that nightmare jolted me from sleep I had failed to realize that the source of my discontent was the relationship I had with my self. The dream forced me to see that achievement had been less a quest to release my true self than an attempt to keep the past buried and unexamined, to deal with it by denying its existence and impact. The legacy of pain, grief, and rage that I carried away with me from home had become an impenetrable barrier, and I could progress no further until I turned and faced the truth of that past.

Confronting the dark corners of the self is truly an awesome task, the thought of which leaves most of us feeling adrift: often helpless, sometimes hopeless, occasionally suicidal, and painfully uncertain about whether we can make the changes demanded by our growth. This dragon wears many guises: amnesia or emotional anesthesia from the trauma of physical, sexual, or psychological abuse; the soul-stunting pattern of the "good girl" who conforms to the needs and expectations of everyone except herself; addictions to food, alcohol, drugs, or relationships; and ignorance or disavowal of one's real talents and abilities, hopes and dreams. Fear of this dragon can trap a woman in an unending race against herself, running from one person to another, from one place to another, from one distraction to another, endlessly searching for herself everywhere but in herself.

The greatest temptation this first dragon presents a

woman is the refusal to look into the depths of herself and a return instead to the familiarity and ignorance of her former life. The pull of old patterns, relationships, life-styles, or addictive distractions can indeed be ferocious, but the quester must move forward even when she wants only to cling to the past. Her weapons against this dragon are hope, perseverance, and an indomitable will. She must believe in herself and her quest even when she feels nothing but doubt; she must continue to hope even when she feels nothing but despair. She must persist even when she wants only to sleep or give up. She must treat herself with compassion even when she is consumed with regret or self-loathing. And perhaps most difficult of all, she must affirm the meaning and purposefulness of her life even when she is experiencing only emptiness and pain.

THE SECOND DRAGON

The second dragon many women must combat is depression. Although certainly not an entity unique to women, it seems a far more common experience among women than men. Often the legacy of abuse or familial dysfunction, the attempt to live life according to the dictates of others, or the struggle against cultural stereotypes that deny women the full range of self-expression, depression can erupt in myriad self-destructive or self-enclosing behaviors. Few women are immune to this dragon, but if viewed as an initiatory challenge on the path to transformation, it can provide a great impetus to healing and change.

Although depression was a formidable obstacle for many women in this book, Annie's experience is prototypical, precipitated by the loss of her mother in childhood, reinforced by her own biological predisposition, compounded by her long-standing uncertainty about what to do with her life, and exacerbated by her enormous awareness of the injustices and cruelties in the world. "I have been depressed on and off probably my entire life," Annie said. "I come from a good, solid genetic pool of depressed people and obviously would have had some kind of tendency toward it. But I think the combination of my mother dying when I was young and some other circumstances in my life resulted in my having depression."

Depression became a foundation, a scaffolding for all of Annie's life experiences. Her mother's death left her feeling abandoned, extremely vulnerable, and responsible for meeting familial emotional needs. After Annie was thrust prematurely into a parental role, her own emotional development was delayed as she strove to be the person she was expected to be rather than the person she might have been had she not become the family caretaker. As a result she became, in her words, a "very good girl," but the price of this role was high, compromising her ability to form intimate friendships and compounding the isolation and loneliness she felt for much of her life. Although many people considered her to be an exceptionally good friend, Annie felt there was no one to whom she could really talk, and only in the last few years has she been able to form close friendships with other women. As so frequently happens with women who labor under the burden of familial expectations or dark secrets, Annie grew up believing that she needed to handle her depression on her own, a belief that prolonged her path to recovery and made her journey more arduous than it might otherwise have been.

"There was a long, long period of time where I just sort of stored everything up, and there probably would have been help there if I had been able to ask for it or accept it," she said. "One of the things I've learned to do is ask for help. I've learned that I truly don't have to do it all alone, and that's been very freeing for me. I spent much of my childhood being told by my grandparents and my father that I was the most beautiful, the brightest, the whatever, and I reacted in two very different ways. One way was to say that there must be something really the matter with me or they wouldn't have to tell me these things all the time. But there was certainly a feeling that I needed to live up to these things. I never believed the physical attributes. I always believed the mental, that I was smart and that I could do whatever I wanted to do. But to me that meant not only being able to read a book and figure out what was going on, but that I was supposed to be able to handle everything alone."

Through a series of positive therapy experiences and an indefatigable commitment to her own healing, Annie was finally able to resolve the loss of her mother and its tempestuous emotional aftermath, thereby freeing herself to develop into her mature self. "I have taken medication on and off for years for depression," she said, "and it took a long time for that to be okay with me because that didn't fit with my being able to handle everything. Once I realized not only that these obstacles were there but that it was okay for them to be there, I started to get better. I think my expectations of myself emotionally, until very recently, just have all been terribly out of whack. Somehow I expected perfection, not intellectually but emotionally. I don't think I saw depression as something I might have to contend with the rest of my life. The turning point came when I finally realized that my depression will get better and worse throughout my life, and that's okay. That's the 'okay' that I didn't have before."

Depression is a complex phenomenon about which much has been written.[3] Regardless of its etiology, it can easily derail a woman, eroding the inner resources upon which she must depend if she is to fulfill her quest. Yet it need not do so. Annie's story illustrates one of the most effective weapons against this particular dragon: the choice to perceive depression not as an indictment of oneself but as a genuine response to emotional, spiritual, and biological pain, and to use it as a catalyst for growth and transformation. "In some ways I would have to say that depression has probably been real good for me," Annie noted. "There were times when I wasn't sure I was going to make it through, but I think it has been an enricher, in a sense. I was always told that you couldn't know what it meant to be really happy unless you'd been really unhappy. And I guess you may not know what it is to be not depressed unless you've been really depressed. And I have been really depressed. But I've always managed to do something. You know, I've never not been able to get out of bed. That may have been all I was able to do, but I could do that."

Twice during the depths of her depression Annie had contemplated suicide, but, she insisted, "I would never act on it. Certainly, during the worst of a couple of depressive episodes I stopped driving the car, and I would imagine that this is connected to the way my mother died. I stopped because I could be driving along and have a clear sense that I could just turn the wheel and go over the bridge, hit a tree, and that would be just fine. But I have not been actively suicidal, probably because I felt it would disappoint everybody around me and because I might miss something if I weren't here. Certainly not from any religious or moral conviction. Now, if I could have arranged to go to sleep for several months, that would have been great, but it wasn't an option. Maybe the most important thing that coming through depression has done for me is that I've realized that while we're all different, basically we're not terribly different from each other. We're unique in our very own ways, but our uniqueness does not make us able to control everything that happens in life. I have always felt different in many ways, one of which has been my depression. But I've learned that I can't fix the world. I have a feeling that I'm not going to be depressed anymore. I don't know that for sure, but I have a feeling that that's not going to happen again because I think I have come a distance I never came before. However, if I'm wrong and I do go through another period of depression, I am convinced that I'll be able to handle it and deal with it and work with what comes afterward. And I don't think that I could always say that."

THE THIRD DRAGON

The third dragon speaks through the voice of every culture that tells women to stay home, be quiet, and be good. This is the dragon of dependence and enclosure, a dragon that socializes us to drift until someone else provides a solution, and to exchange our vitality and independence for a life of safety, passivity, and acquiescence to the status quo.

One of the most tragic messages women receive is that the world does not need our gifts and strengths, that the "real work" is accomplished by men, and that any contribution we might make is peripheral or ancillary. This message is imparted in many ways and from many different sources. Families, for example, often underestimate or ignore the talents and abilities of daughters in favor of sons; as one of my clients once said, "There was only enough money to send one child to school, so my brother got to go even though he couldn't have cared less and I cared immensely." From elementary school through college women are often encouraged by their parents to "get good grades" but rarely given the kind of guidance and support necessary to translate those grades into satisfying lives. Women who pursue various avenues of achievement from politics to the arts are often asked by family members, "When are you going to give this up and get married?" If a woman learns within her own home that her achievement is avocational or secondary to men's, it should come as no surprise if she feels confused, ambivalent, or insecure about developing and utilizing her potential.

Annie spent years feeling deeply dissatisfied with her inability to formulate career goals, a familiar experience in many women's lives. Although she had raised two bright and inquisitive children "with solid values and just enough eccentricity to make it real difficult for them to function in the world," she never saw having and raising children as a goal; instead it had been a normalizing experience, something she felt she was expected to do. She had always had a strong desire to accomplish something more, but she had no idea what that something was supposed to be. "I just didn't know," she remembered wistfully. "I knew I had to do it, whatever 'it' was. There were times that were real despairing and real frightening. I didn't have a goal in the sense that there was something I had to do in the world. I think it's always been that I had to be the best person I could be. But I have always felt there is something there for me to do that I haven't done yet, though it's never been definable." Part of Annie's dilemma arose from the difficulty of choosing which possibility to pursue. She laughed when she remembered completing the research for her doctorate in education. "I took my dissertation off the printer and walked downstairs with it and ripped off the edges and put it on the table and looked at my husband and said, 'Well, can I go to law school now?' And he asked me if I would wait a little while."

Educational experiences can intensify the confusing messages many of us receive from home. Researchers Sally Reis and Carolyn Callahan[4] and Lee Anne Bell[5] found that young women at all grade levels are most often praised in school for sitting in the front row, and their work is rewarded for neatness and form rather than originality and substance. Further, they are often criticized for displaying the very qualities for which young men are rewarded, qualities such as assertiveness, creativity, analytical ability, and nontraditional approaches to learning and problem solving.

Young women drawn to nontraditional fields are still advised by some teachers and counselors that those careers are inappropriate for females. And because women are seldom expected to be financially responsible for their own lives, they are less likely to receive the kind of academic preparation or career counseling that would enable them to compete in an increasingly complex society. Consequently, many find themselves as adults trapped in low-paying clerical or service-related jobs regardless of their intelligence or range of ability. Others relinquish themselves to dysfunctional or unsatisfying relationships because they do not believe they can function effectively alone, or because they lack the necessary job skills to support themselves or their children.

Many women are socialized to hide their talents and skills so as not to threaten people in authority or frighten prospective partners away. They are taught to be (or appear to be) less intelligent, less competent, and less mature than they actually are, to be less educated, and to interrupt their careers when the demands of their partners and/or children interfere. Positing affiliation as antithetical to achievement and independence places many women in a terrible position. A promising Hispanic mathematics student whom I once counseled felt a terrible pressure to drop out of college after a particularly successful quarter during which she was rejected by young men in her ethnic group. She also remembered her mother warning her that she would have to downplay or abandon her talent and ambition if she ever wished to marry. Some women give up on themselves in order to keep the love and affection of others, a choice that can have devastating consequences for the women and the people they love. Kristen, a twin growing up in an extremely close family, knew she had to separate from that closeness so that she could form her own sense of self, even though that decision was very painful. "Being able to have an individual personality or identity and being able to really maintain that while maintaining close family relationships was, and remains, one of my most difficult challenges."

Some women attempt to arrest their own development because the idea of growing up and taking responsibility for their own lives is too frightening. And sometimes women enter into marriages or relationships not as avenues for individuation and fulfillment but to forestall the anxiety of discovering their own paths by substituting their own goals and dreams with a partner's. But the consequences of such decisions can be very sad, leaving a woman's life devoid of her own vital presence.

When Sarah was informed of her mother's institutionalization for mental illness, she was devastated. In order to live with this knowledge she closed herself down, refusing to show what feelings she allowed herself to feel and questioning the wisdom of becoming an adult. "I remember telling myself, I have to grow up but I don't really want to grow up if I have to be like my mother. And I did not want to, so that's the point at which I decided to stay a little girl." This decision led to an early marriage in which she followed and supported her husband as he pursued his career interests in the ministry and social work. But while her marriage temporarily displaced her need to create a viable life for herself, it only postponed the inevitable.

"I got married at twenty-one," Sarah recalled. "I was married for eleven years and was very dissatisfied for the last few of them. I had no sense of self because my first husband and I did the same type of work and he was more or less the leader. I would go along and do things with him, but I didn't really have a sense of what kinds of things I wanted to do away from him." Eventually Sarah realized that she could no longer live in her husband's shadow. "If I wanted to feel any confidence in myself or experience any success in life, I needed to leave that relationship and find out who I was."

Women who work outside their homes, particularly in nontraditional fields where there are few women (like science, engineering, and the trades), are likely to encounter this dragon in one of its many forms, including isolation, sexual harassment, and the lack of mentoring and community. Those with children often find few support systems—child care, flexible schedules, or alternative achievement paths—that would enable them to thrive. And many struggle to find a balance between their own needs and those of their children.

Melia winced as she recalled the time when two of her sons were under the age of four and she was struggling to balance motherhood and her career as a nurse practitioner. She described being wracked with guilt and pain because she knew full well the consequences of poor parenting as well as not using one's abilities to the fullest. "I was unable to make a choice," she said. "If I gave up my career, which I had worked so hard to build up, I would have to start again. And that's so scary because whatever progress I had made I didn't want to lose. I thought, I'm already thirty-two; it's harder to get back into my field if you're a woman, if you're Asian, and you're not a medical doctor. To just give that up and be a full-time mom is so scary. But when I'm at work I think of my kids, how they don't have me, and that's so painful. I hear my patients talking about deprivation and abandonment from their parents, and here I am working and listening to them, and my own kids are over there with a sitter. So that was a very difficult time for me. I had to make a choice. My husband was supportive of whatever I wanted to do, so it wasn't him that was keeping me from choosing. It was not a question of whether I would be a mom or have a career; I had to find a way to blend both."

How does one meet the very difficult challenges presented by this dragon? I believe there are three interrelated attitudes that women must cultivate. The first requires us to take our own lives seriously and teach our daughters to do the same, acknowledging that regardless of whether we marry or remain single, we alone are responsible for creating our lives. Second, we must not substitute protection from others for pursuit of our own goals and dreams. Instead we must recognize and assert the validity and primacy of our own needs. Only by doing this will we stop reacting to societal constraints and start creating and defining ourselves for ourselves. Only then will we empower ourselves and each other to integrate those needs into the totality of our personal and professional lives.

Third, we must be willing to face squarely and face down the fears and anxieties we encounter as we seek to master these challenges. These fears—fear of isolation and abandonment, fear of rejection, fear of disapproval, fear of failure—are neither insubstantial nor unfounded. All women who defy cultural stereotypes or patriarchal taboos will find themselves at times in physical or psychological danger; as I learned only too painfully, the price of leaving home can be very high indeed. But as Carolyn Heilbrun so eloquently expressed,

> We women have lived too much with closure: "If he notices me, if I marry him, if I get into college, if I get this work accepted, if I get that job"—there always seems to loom the possibility of something being over, settled, sweeping clear the way for contentment. This is the delusion of a passive life. When the hope for closure is abandoned, when there is an end to fantasy, adventure for women will begin. Endings . . . are for romance or for day-dreams, but not for life.[6]

THE FOURTH DRAGON

A fourth dragon along the heroic journey reveals itself as the hydra-headed demon of prejudice, which tells women they cannot have great desires or great possibilities because they are female. Exclusion from the challenge of the heroic quest goes beyond the mere fact of gender; it is augmented by an array of cultural demons that dismiss women if they do not conform to stereotypical criteria of age, attractiveness, or size and who marginalize women further if they are of color, have disabilities, or are lesbian. Several of my clients have wrestled with the complex issue of weight, wanting to overcome compulsive eating disorders but feeling angry and ambivalent about societal attitudes that condemn women to ridicule and invisibility if they dare to be large. Even women who do not struggle with weight issues often have great difficulty perceiving themselves as capable or worthy of success because they do not conform to prescribed standards of beauty and personality for women.[7] Forged through centuries of misogyny, discrimination, and victimization, this dragon is particularly insidious because it is ubiquitous, often unconsciously internalized, and highly resistant to change.

Despite her longstanding rebellion against her culture's attitudes toward women, Melia's movement into greater visibility within the health care community made her aware of the extent to which she had internalized some of these beliefs. Over the past several years she has often been invited to lecture before groups of nursing and medical students, and she recently organized an innovative symposium for interdisciplinary health care personnel. But these accomplishments exacerbated the guilt and shame she quite often felt in the presence of men, especially when she assumed a leadership role. "In my country," she said, "women were not allowed or encouraged to speak in front of groups of men, especially if that involved teaching or lecturing. As a woman, standing in front of men and teaching them gives me a wonderful feeling of accomplishment, but afterward I don't want to accept the credit if anybody praises me. The act of doing the work is wonderful. But if I get any praise, I'd rather give it to my husband or another team member who is a man. In my culture women do the work, but they are in the background and credit is given to men. And I do that. I do all the hard work but then I say that it's my husband's idea or acknowledge someone else. It's almost a habit. I catch myself saying it and then I stop myself, but the praise is hard to receive, and I make excuses for my competence. I cannot just say 'thank you.' There's a certain shame I always feel in rejecting the traditions I was brought up to obey."

The decision to reject cultural stereotypes about life-style, appearance, or aspiration is not easily made. Most, if not all, cultures discourage women from the full exercise of their capacities or the full development of their potentials, so when we do attempt to do so we are often perceived as deviant or unusual. Even as girls are exhorted to do well in school, they are also criticized by some family members, teachers, or peers for appearing too bright, too accomplished, too successful, or too different, and many are warned that divergence from cultural norms will result in loneliness and ostracism. Along with most of the women with whom I have worked, I can recall painful experiences of being isolated, rejected, or punished for not being "like everyone else," and many of us learn to put aside our hopes and dreams, often at great cost to our sanity and well-being.

Societal conditioning to be silent and invisible, to conform to stereotypes or rigid role expectations, can easily lead to what Harriet Goldhor Lerner calls "de-selfing."[8] Women share a common history of being labelled as "shrill," "shrewish," "unfeminine," or "crazy" for speaking out against oppression and injustice, stereotyped as "incompetent" and "hysterical" if they attempt difficult or dangerous tasks, and ridiculed for rebelling against the norm. As Lerner says, "Unlike our male heroes, who fight and even die for what they believe in, women may be condemned for waging a bloodless and humane revolution for their own rights."[9]

But women can refuse to hide themselves away even when the consequences are severe. Coming out as a lesbian was an extremely frightening experience for Leah, profoundly altering her relationship with her family as well as her career plans. "I always felt weird on the outside," she remembered. "What I now know was that my being a budding lesbian gave me a sense of enormous outsideness. I didn't quite fit. I didn't understand the other girls. I didn't get what they were up to. I didn't get boys. I didn't get makeup. And the fact that I didn't get it didn't feel good. It wasn't until the light came on that it became clear to me what was happening."

Leah's relations with her parents were shattered when they learned of their daughter's lesbianism. "My family was incredibly rejecting and angry. Things were not good before that. I had been kicked out of the house as a teenager for behaving heterosexually, which I find hilariously funny. My father searched my room, found a pack of birth control pills, and a great storm emerged. And he said, 'We're paying for you, you'll do what we tell you.' I said, 'It's my body, I'll do what I like.' He said, 'Take your body and get out of here.' " Although her parents had always encouraged their children to be independent thinkers, this encouragement did not hold where their daughter's sexuality was concerned. "My parents had always said don't be sheep and follow the flock; what they did not say was follow *our* flock. So I didn't." Because she refused to compromise her values or integrity for her parents' financial support, Leah was forced to leave home at seventeen, in the middle of her first year of college. "I had worked before," she said. "Now I just worked more." Despite the successes and accomplishments she would later accrue, her efforts to reconcile with her parents were spurned, and their rejection continues to this day, some twenty years later.

Parental antipathy was not the only manifestation of this dragon in her life. As she discovered the truth of her sexual orientation Leah was confronted with her own internalized preconceptions and fears. With the support of an older friend she was able to dislodge their choke hold and free herself to integrate her lesbian feminism with her desire to become a psychologist. But formulating her career goals brought her face to face with cultural homophobia. "This was in 1972," she recalled. "It was not a time when there were lesbian psychologists out in the world. I was scared to death." Her apprehension almost prevented her from applying to graduate school because she was warned that she would be refused entry or expelled if her lesbianism were to become known. Even after she completed her degree and became an assistant professor of psychology at a large public university, her commitment to understanding gay and lesbian issues precluded a career in academic psychology. "I would have enjoyed being an academic," she said, "but I was told, 'Look, you do research in lesbian issues, you can't get tenure with that.' I was grateful to the person who was honest with me and told me that. He was right. I look in triumph, however, at the fact that the current chair of the clinical department and the director of the psychology clinic are both lesbian. Some of that does have to do with my influence and my being willing to be an 'out' lesbian in that department and to show them just how valuable I was even after I became a clinical faculty member."

Racial discrimination, yet another facet of this particular dragon, is one of the most ubiquitous and demanding challenges for women of color; as Kristen said, "I can never just be good enough in and of myself." Although prejudice was no stranger in her life, its presence became more onerous after she graduated from high school and entered college. Suddenly she found herself in a highly competitive environment, one in which she lost confidence in herself as an equally competent student. "Most minorities feel some insecurity about how they got to where they are, that maybe they only got there because they are a certain racial group and someone's trying to fill a quota," she said. Once she realized that she really was as intelligent and capable as the next person, Kristen was able to perform quite well. But racism is a force with which she will always contend.

Kristen described some of the ways in which this dragon assails her professional life. "There is a reality that people will latch onto any qualified person of color they can find. And sometimes it's hard to let people know that they must look beyond your race and look at who you are. That is very difficult because people tend to pigeonhole you." She has often found herself occupying the position of "token minority," a stressful experience in which her performance is evaluated not solely on its own but as representative of an entire group of people. In such a situation, she said, there is little room for error or mistakes. "If I make a mistake it's not just a mistake for myself but for all minority people. I find myself in the position of having to defend people of other races and cultures, of always being a spokesperson for the oppressed minorities, more so in a city like this than in a bigger city where there are more people of color in responsible positions. People tend to have lower expectations if you're a person of color. And therefore you have to really impress upon them first, that your standards are much higher than that, and second, that they have to look at that. This is particularly difficult for someone like me who is light-skinned, because people can choose to ignore the racial issue if they want to. They can look at me and say, well, she's white, or she's Jewish. And there are other instances where people will say, 'We have a racially diverse staff because we have Kristen here. And look what a wonderful job she's doing.' "

The interaction of gender and race complicates this picture. "It is difficult enough being female and having bosses who are male," Kristen observed, "because they expect a lower standard of work from women and so they don't appreciate a truly exceptional job that a woman is performing. But the situation gets worse when you start adding factors of race. As a result I have to be much more serious than I would otherwise be. It is not relaxing. I feel like I have to do everything exceptionally well and that if I don't I'll be dismissed or excused as 'just a black female.' I don't know whether being a black female is three times worse than being a white female. I kind of doubt that it is, although I have seen white women who are doing work like mine and seem to have an easier time of it because people relate to them in a more serious way. But it's harder for me to think about sexism in relation to myself. I think sexism is a real thing, but it's further away from me than racism is."

It takes enormous courage for women to confront this fourth dragon in whatever form it appears. This is not the false courage of bravado or denial but the courage of deep and determined self-knowledge and an unflinching awareness of this dragon's existence. From such fortitude can evolve a constellation of inner resources that empower and enable our continued resistance. In analyzing the lives of thirty-five eminent women, Barbara Kerr[10] enumerated several of these qualities. She found, for example, that the women in her study were safeguarded by their ability to be alone, whether that quality derived from individual preference or harsh circumstance. Not only did this permit them to develop and nurture their intellect and skills, it also helped free them from the potent influence of negative stereotypes. Another critical inner resource is what Kerr called "thorns and shells"; that is, most of the women in her study had molded a psychological armor around themselves that permitted them to engage in the world while protecting the integrity of their inner selves from whatever obstacle might be thrown in their path. Further, each refused to acknowledge the limitations of gender, thereby assuming "a stance of equality with men even when faced with strong resistance."[11]

Leah's reflections upon her own ability to contend with this dragon reinforce Kerr's findings. "There's a Yiddish word, *achshan*, that my Zaddi, my father's father, used to talk about when he was an old man. My family are all *achshan*, we're all very stubborn people. We are persistent, we don't give up, we doggedly pursue things, we're self-righteous, which in some ways is a strength as well as a vulnerability. We believe in what we believe. We think we're right. And that's been helpful for me. I thought I was right. I didn't have any major doubts about the rightness of my beliefs, the rightness of my choices. I get scared about how people will respond, particularly to my being a lesbian. I'm afraid that people are going to hate me. So I say, 'Oh well, so they will.' And that's been a real resource."

While a strong sense of self is a primary means of defense against this dragon, it is insufficient unless accompanied by a clear recognition of the ways in which women's lives are shaped and distorted by discriminatory beliefs, attitudes, traditions, and myths. The work of attribution theorists such as Carol Dweck and Barbara Licht strongly suggests that women take far too much responsibility for cultural oppression, translating "lack of opportunity" into "lack of ability," and "effortful success" into "luck or chance."[12] An essential component in a woman's arsenal of dragon-slaying weapons is the ability to externalize prejudice and cultural oppression in whatever form they appear, to see these forces as emanating from the larger society rather than as indictments of her own shortcomings. The dragon of prejudice and discrimination—sexism, racism, ageism, ableism, homophobia, and weight oppression—takes a tremendous toll on women's self-confidence, self-esteem, and self-expression. Unless women develope a solid core of inner strength, this dragon will irrevocably suppress the pursuit of our quests.

THE FIFTH DRAGON

The fifth dragon is the tendency to say yes to too many expectations and demands, often at the expense of our own physical, psychological, and spiritual well-being. Most women have a very difficult time establishing effective boundaries that protect our energies and enable us to achieve a balance between caring for ourselves and caring for others. As a result, a serious illness or emotional breakdown is often the catalyst that compels us to realize the immense importance of mastering this dragon.

After a long and prominent career as an educator, administrator, and community activist, Joan was hospitalized for exhaustion and burnout. This was an excruciatingly painful experience during which she realized that she had never learned to acknowledge and honor her own limitations. "For so many years my whole person in lots of ways was suppressed by who I was as a Sister and by an expectation of my competency. I was a really good teacher, a good administrator of a great school, well liked in the parish. I had a lot of skills and talents as a helper and a leader, and I had never really failed until I became ill." As a youngster in Montana Joan had been a competitive skier, a slalom racer. "Skiing was a symbol for me of being very competent, very much an achiever, of 'the sky's the limit.' I saw myself as a person who was not vulnerable, who is successful and achieving and a rescuer. My burnout made me realize that not recognizing my own limitations realistically made me my own worst obstacle."

Once in the hospital, she said, she posed a very difficult challenge for those responsible for assisting her recovery. "I was the hardest person for anybody to work with. They had a terrible time peeling off my veneer and getting down to where I could be angry, face who I really was without a role, and accept any kind of vulnerability in myself. I was humiliated that I was in a psychiatric ward. It was terribly difficult to come to grips with the person I was and the person I was reduced to because I was in a ward surrounded by people who had all kinds of serious problems. People living on the streets who were suicidal, people who had lots of money but were manic-depressive, women who had gone into deep depressions when their husbands dropped dead, teenagers who were suffering from anorexia and attempted suicide and all sorts of things. But my own addictions had brought me there; my own self-destructiveness in overwork had brought me to that point. And it was very good for me because I became aware that this was a time in my life to make some choices, that I had only so many years left to give, that my energies were not going to be endless and limitless."

Leah also came upon this dragon when she least expected to meet it. By the time she was thirty-five she had become a successful psychologist, managing a private practice and building an international reputation as a scholar, activist, and theorist in the field of feminist therapy. But seemingly overnight she developed a degenerative nerve disease that paralyzed her vocal cords; what began as a slight case of laryngitis left her, within three months, unable to talk. Her condition, she was told, was permanent and untreatable, and she was devastated. "I use my voice to work and my voice to live, plus I was in such a bad spasm that I stopped being able to breathe well," she said. Although she could talk with the aid of an electronic larynx, her ability to breathe began to fail, and for two weeks she was so ill that she could neither get out of bed nor eat. Her larynx was wracked with spasms of such magnitude that they triggered asthma, the medication for which only made the spasms worse. Leah was plunged into deep despair; for a time it seemed certain that she would have to give up her work and her livelihood, if indeed she survived the disease at all.

In desperation she sought alternative forms of medical treatment and slowly, miraculously regained her ability to speak and to breathe. "But it really brought me up short, to put it mildly," she said, "because I now have this chronic illness. I've relapsed once; I might again. I always have it with me; I'm always aware of the spasticity in my throat, larynx, and tongue. And it made me evaluate what I was doing, particularly the pace at which I was leading my life. Believe it or not, I have slowed down. I've become much better about taking time. I'm much more willing to say I can't. To say no. It was sort of this great confrontation with the limits of my physical capacities. I think I am more distant than I used to be; I put out less energy than I did. I don't think I'm a worse therapist, but I'm definitely much more clear and protective about my own energy boundaries. I don't go so many extra miles anymore, and still I think I'm a very giving, available therapist. I'm more willing to say I can't do this, or I don't want to do that, or this time and space are sacred to me and I won't give them away. And before that I would say yes to everything, all the time. I just took everything on."

Leah's life reminded me of a jingle for a perfume commercial that aired on television many years ago. A beautiful and impeccably groomed woman cooked a substantial breakfast for her family of four before dashing off to a full day of executive responsibilities, then rushed home to dress alluringly for an evening out with her husband. Throughout the commercial the woman sang an inane song extolling her ability to handle all these demands and responsibilities with aplomb, " 'cause I'm a WOMAN . . ." That commercial is the quintessential portrait of this dragon, an image that women who choose nontraditional lives frequently are exhorted to emulate. But as most of us have discovered or will one day learn, it just doesn't work.

In a previous research study[13] I asked more than one hundred women what they considered to be their major life stresser; the overwhelming majority said that achieving balance among work, relationships, and time alone to develop their own selves was their most difficult challenge. It is very hard for women to attain this balance because all women are expected to assume domestic burdens not assumed by most men. Additionally, those who act as trailblazers in their professional lives are expected to embrace the male model of achievement and success, an inherently unhealthy model that leaves us exhausted in body and spirit, isolated, alienated, and disconnected from ourselves and each other. Mastering this dragon is not a simple matter of saying, "I can't do it all"; more significantly, it demands that we say, "I won't."

Although not extolled in any myth, limit setting is a formidable and heroic challenge because a woman must insist upon her right to choose when and how she will respond to the people, institutions, and situations in her life. Self-insistence is not something most women are taught or encouraged to pursue, but once learned it empowers us to affirm ourselves, define our own boundaries, and shape both the direction and intensity of our lives on a moment-by-moment basis. It releases us from the obligation to say yes to every request that comes along and reminds us that sometimes the most self-affirming thing we can do is say no. No to a telephone call we are too tired to answer; no to a request for time when we have no more to give; no to an expectation that we ceaselessly care for others at the expense of ourselves; no to an expectation that we work full time both inside and outside the home with insufficient participation by our partners; no to a patriarchal concept of achievement and success that extols autonomy, competition, and power at the expense of connection, cooperation, and partnership; no to the denial, evaluation, or sacrifice of the feminine in favor of the wholesale incorporation of masculine values and attributes.

Whether we are deciding to ascend the ladder of public success, to balance motherhood and career, or to answer the telephone, limit setting is a skill women cannot afford to ignore. Far too many women run too hard for too long on too few reserves for too much of their lives, racing from one demand or activity to another until, our spirits spent, we succumb to depression, illness, addiction, or burnout. I have listened to countless women castigate themselves for being "selfish" when they attended to their own needs before those of others. Yet without allowing themselves the "self"-ishness to determine when and how much to give and to whom, women will continue to sacrifice their personal and professional effectiveness upon the altar of this dragon.

Although the demands and complexities of daily life are unlikely to diminish, women can change the way we relate to those demands. We can remind ourselves and each other that the challenges we face in setting effective limits are universal, that the "superwoman" ethos is inherently misogynistic, and that we must not accept the exhaustion of our bodies, minds, and spirits as the price we must pay for participating in the world. And we can remind ourselves that we cannot fix that world. I have known many women whose sensitivity to injustice and enormous awareness of the complex problems facing our planet left them feeling helpless, overwhelmed, and in despair. No one by herself can save the world. But if we can come to terms with this most painful realization we can free ourselves to do what we can wherever we can, however great or small our contribution may prove to be.

When Annie confronted this dragon a huge piece of her depression fell away. "I'm just starting to get this sorted out, but I'm realizing that there are some things you can't do anything about—that are just going to be that way. Just last week I was having a conversation where I made the comment that people could well look back on this era of ours and say that it was the Dark Ages—that people are bashing each other up on the streets and brutalizing women and children. It's awful and depressing and horrible. But I've come to a place where I think I can work around little bits of it, and that's all I can do. I can be decent to the people around me, which I've always tried to do. I can volunteer in certain areas, I can apply myself in certain ways, but I cannot change everything myself. I think part of what I suffered from for a long, long time was being told there wasn't anything that I wanted to do that I couldn't do. That's not a favor to anybody because there are lots of things I want to do that I can't do. I have always felt that the world was a very terrifying, uncertain place and the fact that I couldn't control it meant there was something wrong with me. Now I know it doesn't mean that there's something wrong with me. It just means that I'm like everybody else. And you know, close to fifty, I think I've finally figured that out. So hopefully the next however many years are going to be a little less frustrating."

As more women move into positions of power and influence, as we penetrate domains historically reserved for men, we have a rare opportunity to create a world order imbued with the values and skills women have honed over centuries: caring, cooperation, community, and compassion. In recognizing the validity of our own needs and the necessity of honoring them, in learning the art of setting limits in our personal lives, we empower ourselves to set limits in the larger world and to radically reshape the world along more humane, supportive, and responsive dimensions.

THE SIXTH DRAGON

It is the rare woman who does not encounter this last dragon at least once in her life. This is the dragon of unexpected hardship and loss, a dragon that roars into a woman's life with sudden and devastating force, tearing apart the fabric of her life, challenging her physical, emotional, and spiritual resources to the utmost and jeopardizing both her physical and psychological health. Catastrophic illness, the death or collapse of an important relationship, the disintegration of a way of life—these are but three of the myriad manifestations of this particular dragon. This dragon rarely appears as an isolated event; meeting its challenges successfully requires a resolve and inner strength equal to the maelstrom it creates.

The Lebanese civil war brought an inconceivable level of terror and brutality into everyday life in Beirut, systematically destroying its people and its institutions. Surrounded by shocked and terrified family members and neighbors, confronted on a daily basis with friends who were alive in the morning and dead by afternoon, Zena witnessed the disintegration of her community and its entire way of life. Although she was able to escape the physical presence of the war through foreign study, the emotional impact permeated her life.

For years she had been able to console herself and persevere because of her deep underlying belief that the war must be happening for a reason even if she had no idea what that reason was. But when her beloved youngest brother was killed by a sniper's bullet this belief collapsed, and she was overwhelmed with feelings of vulnerability, chaos, and meaninglessness. "I think it's really the loss of a child that gives you a sense of meaninglessness," Zena observed. "You can always justify why an adult person lost his or her life after they have lived and fulfilled some of their dreams, but for a child to be born and then not fulfill anything and die at the age of eight or nine, it doesn't make any sense. And my being here and my parents and brother being there added to this awareness of how vulnerable everything is, how quickly you can lose someone you love."

Shortly after her brother's death Zena married an American and was advised by friends to give up her student visa in exchange for the green card to which she was now entitled. This advice was to have disastrous consequences. Despite her marriage, her status as an exchange student left her ineligible to apply for permanent residency until she had fulfilled the American immigration policy requiring all foreign students to return to their home countries for a period of two years following completion of their studies. Zena was in a terrible bind: She had to go home in order to renew her student visa, but both the American Embassy in Beirut and the airport had been closed. Even if she could find her way to Lebanon, she had no hope of securing a visa and thus no hope of reentering this country. But if she stayed in the United States without a visa she was in imminent danger of being deported.

Zena and her husband filed an appeal which, they were told, had virtually no chance of being granted; nevertheless, it might forestall deportation proceedings while a decision was pending. Although threatened with displacement before her doctoral work was completed, a situation complicated by the increasingly erratic financial support from her government, Zena still had to perform academically. "The university wasn't going to wait for me. I had to wake up every day and do the work I was supposed to do. And every day I woke up thinking, 'Oh, probably I should have died in my sleep,' because graduate school was too much to deal with on top of the worry about my parents and their safety. The events in Lebanon were terribly traumatic. Losing friends, seeing people dying, seeing horrors. There is nothing—no dissertation, no deportation, nothing—that could compare. But still I had to perform. This was a period that was very challenging to go through and to go through gracefully."

The cumulative stress took its toll; a series of mysterious illnesses eroded Zena's health, and for a period of time she felt certain she would not survive without sustaining serious emotional or physical damage. The immigration appeal dragged on for several years, enabling Zena to complete her dissertation and graduate, but another year would pass before she learned that her appeal had inexplicably been granted. Forced into inactivity during this year because she could not work without a permit, Zena lived in fear of imminent deportation with little to distract her from the uncertainty and anxiety of the future.

Lesser challenges would lead many individuals to give up. As I watched Zena move through those harrowing years I often wondered how she was able to survive with her sanity intact. Yet she had done more than survive; she had retained and deepened her warmth, compassion, humor, and humanity. "I could have given up," she said, "that is true. It doesn't mean that sometimes the thought doesn't come to my mind. What keeps me going is the thought that life is a play in which I have a role, and I'm going to exit at some point. Also, the people who love me and the people I love would be extremely hurt if I collapsed.

"When I think about life in general," she continued, "I know I have seen the ugliest face of it. Once I heard my thoughts articulated on a program about evil by a man named Philip Holly. He said, 'Think about it like a big hurricane, and in the middle there is the eye of the hurricane, and if you're in the eye sometimes you can see a little bit of blue sky. The idea is to stretch that little bit of blue sky as much as you can.' And I always think about my life in terms of that little bit of blue sky in the middle of the hurricane. You stretch it as much as you can for yourself, and for the sake of the people you love, and for the sake of whatever hope exists. Sometimes I feel it is getting bigger and sometimes smaller, but I work for it. In spite of everything that's awful there's a part of me that doesn't want to give up. I don't know why there is that part of me; it's deep within, and it remains confident that I can pass through it. Sometimes I feel that I'm going to lose this confidence if more people in my life get hurt or something really meaningful to me is lost. So far I haven't lost hope. So far there is something powerful inside that says, 'You can go through it.' "

Many years ago, when searching for ways to comprehend how I had survived the severe dysfunction in my own family, I came across a remarkable series of longitudinal studies conducted by Norman Garmezy, Auke Tellegen, and their colleagues at the University of Minnesota.[14] "Project Competence" had meticulously probed the personality and coping strategies of children who were exposed to prolonged and extremely stressful familial or environmental conditions but who prevailed by developing what these researchers described as extraordinary competence. Several qualities were identified as critical factors in children's ability to defy the odds and emerge with their spirits and psyches intact; of these, three were considered especially important: intelligence, emotional flexibility, and the ability to identify, reach toward, and make full use of love and support wherever it appeared. I was fascinated by this research because I felt a deep resonance with its findings, and because I recognized that many of the women I interviewed for this book had these special qualities. But it seemed to me that there was something far more profound at work. Intellectual and emotional resources are critical strengths to summon in coping with this dragon, but they do not explain how some individuals exposed to highly traumatic life events weave those experiences into highly functional lives while others succumb to psychological impairment, self-destruction, or sociopathy. The missing variable in this complex equation is, I believe, the ability to perceive and draw upon a strong nucleus of spiritual strength.

Spirituality, which I define as the state of being profoundly in touch with our own inner being or with the Creator, is not something many people feel comfortable talking about outside the confines of their particular religious traditions or communities. It is also something that makes the majority of psychiatrists, psychologists, and mental health professionals especially nervous. In part this discomfort stems from the fact that there is no commonly agreed upon language for describing spiritual experiences. Many labels are used, but the experience itself is excruciatingly difficult to describe. What language is used is often emotionally charged and unavoidably influenced by our cultural or religious backgrounds, rendering communication difficult, at times impossible. Moreover, a spiritual event is such a radical departure from our ordinary state of consciousness, and it conflicts so powerfully with the dominant Western view of reality, that most people do not discuss their experiences for fear of being labelled "crazy."

But these experiences are much more common than is ordinarily thought, and they are far from crazy. Abraham Maslow[15] was convinced that all people have the capacity for encountering spiritual reality, a belief with which I completely concur. There are estimates from research studies that at least 30 percent of adults in our society have had some type of powerful spiritual experience, but my own previous research suggests that the incidence is much higher.[16] I have also found such experiences to be common among people who are considered gifted or highly capable and among my psychotherapy clients, especially when they are integrating painful memories or embarking upon new goals or life directions. Although spiritual experiences are generally viewed by mental health professionals as symptomatic of psychopathology, the evidence suggests that quite the opposite is true. Spiritual experiences often act as powerful catalysts for change, giving rise to a renewed sense of hope, meaning, and purpose in life, a deepening of significant values, and a permanent transformation of the psyche in the direction of wholeness and health.[17]

An individual can tap into her spiritual core in a variety of ways including dream states, fasting, listening to music, or contemplating a work of art. It can be triggered by exercise, fatigue, meditation, illness, or the survival of clinical death, or it can be sought through a myriad of spiritual disciplines that have evolved over centuries. Regardless of how we encounter our spirituality, each of us interprets that reality in our own unique way. For Zena it is a "little bit of blue sky" that reminds her, in the depths of crisis, of her ability to survive the fires of a particular initiation. When I was a child I had several powerful dreams in which a "guardian angel" would offer the comfort and reassurance I desperately needed to marshal my will and fight to preserve myself. In later years this guidance continued to make its presence felt in dreams or meditative states, encouraging me to look beyond the surface for deeper levels of meaning and strength, occasionally suggesting alternative courses of action, and always reminding me that I could grow from every experience if I would determine to do so. I did not always appreciate this advice, but it always turned out to be right.

Debra remembered a powerful event that altered the course of her life. Some time ago she was thrown from a river raft into icy water at the top of a treacherous series of rapids. "I knew I could die on the spot," she said. "I contemplated just giving up. I had been depressed and semisuicidal, but I realized that life was just too damn interesting to let it go, and I wanted to see how it all came out. I also learned that everything I thought I knew about water was wrong and that I'd have to work *with* the river and use every trick I could think of to survive intact. It was a great metaphor for life."

To cope with her illness, Leah experimented with a variety of alternative medical treatments, one of which entailed a kind of "laying on of hands" by a spiritual healer. This treatment not only contributed to her recovery but opened her up to dealing with her spirituality for the first time in her life. "It's not as if I've become someone who clearly is heavily into being spiritual," she said. "I don't think that will ever be the case for me. I'm too much my father's daughter. I'm too much the rationalist. And yet I'm more aware of the uncontrollable, the unpredictable, the mysterious, the things that may be."

Why is it important to summon one's spiritual resources when contending with the sixth dragon? I believe there are several compelling reasons. First, they enable an individual to believe in a greater meaning, purpose, and wholeness to life than can be seen from the limited vantage point of human consciousness. Such a belief significantly boosts a person's commitment to learn from whatever she is passing through, and it strengthens the inner muscles she must use to avoid the victimization that often attends adversity. Spiritual resources also help her realize that an individual can be caught up in terrible circumstances that she can neither control nor fully comprehend, without being to blame for their occurrence.

Second, they enable her to live more fully in the present moment. Leah's words are instructive here. "I think my illness has made me appreciate everything differently. *Grateful* is a word I never used very much, and it's a word I use a lot now. I have a sense of gratitude for all the things I took for granted, like the simple act of talking, being able to move my mouth in the morning and have sound come out. And that has changed my relationship to the world, not in a way I can easily describe. It's interesting. I've always been aware of how unpredictable life is. You grow up Jewish and you learn Jewish history and you really get a sense that things can be good, and then a new anti-Semitic tyrant can come along and everything is lost. And I always knew that intellectually. I think emotionally that has gotten integrated into this whole things-could-change-at-any-minute phenomenon. It's made me more appreciative of what I have, to not take it for granted. Getting sick made me more aware on a gut level, an emotional level, of how nothing is permanent, how everything is temporary. And therefore you must enjoy the now as much as you possibly can." Out of the ability to be present in the present comes an attentiveness to intuitive wisdom and an openness to new possibilities, new directions, and new ways of responding to the situations or circumstances in which we find ourselves.

Finally, and perhaps most important, activating our spiritual awareness reminds us that this dragon can never be vanquished in its entirety while we are still residents of planet Earth. As Judith Viorst sums up so clearly in the title of her book, life is a series of "necessary losses."[18] Some are relatively mild, while others carry a force of devastating magnitude. By drawing upon our profound inner resources we can live more fully in the presence of this dragon and move beyond passivity, bitterness, grief, and despair to acceptance, transformation, and wholeness.

The task of becoming a fully functioning female human being is complex, the dragons legion. At every step along the way we must challenge those stereotypes, fears, and taboos that enclose our possibilities, tempt us back to sleep, or limit our involvement in the affairs of the world. We must refuse to hide or to see ourselves as inadequate or inferior, refuse to trade our dreams for the dubious security of patriarchal protection, and refuse to collude in the suppression or exploitation of women—or men. We must assert the validity of our perceptions and needs and recognize that, as Jessie Barnard said, we "have as much right to define the human situation as men do, that [we] do not have to accept the male definition of everything, and that as human beings—diverse, heterogeneous, variegated—[we] are deserving in [our] own right, and that [we] do not have to be like men to be worthy."[19]

The Grail of wholeness is hard won. At any point along the way we can stumble and fall, but we fail in our quest only if we fail to pick ourselves up and try again. The initiation may demand more from us more often than we ever thought possible, but it "offers the female hero the opportunity to develop qualities such as courage, skill, and independence, which would atrophy in a protected environment. Such qualities do not spring full blown from the hero's head, but are developed as responses to the demands and challenges of experience."[20] And women become heroes when we confront the dragons in our path and slowly, inexorably subdue them.

CHAPTER FOUR

Allies of
All Seasons

W hen Zena entered graduate school at Lebanese University in her early twenties, she came in contact with a professor who became extremely important in her life. She was unlike any woman Zena had ever known before, an intelligent, well-educated, and independent woman in her late thirties who was single, had no children, and lived a nontraditional life in a highly traditional culture. "She was a woman who chose not to conform," Zena remarked, her voice growing stronger with her memories. "And since she was older than I it gave me hope that I could be a nonconformist. She and I used to discuss our state as women. We questioned the status quo, the hurdles we were encountering in our university life, she as a professor with brand-new ideas and I as a graduate student trying to study and do some practicum with other people. You know, I remember her because she wasn't related to me. I always thought that because my mom and I are related by blood it was her duty to love and support me because I'm her daughter. Now this woman was not related to me; she had no family duty to support me. She just had this intellectual duty as a professor to be my mentor, and that meant a lot to me. I felt like there was hope. There was a light at the end of the tunnel. There were people who were going to be like me, who thought like me but at a higher level. Her thoughts and her personality were by then pretty developed and sophisticated, and I looked up to her.

"She had come from doing a doctorate in France with totally and radically different ideas about how science should be taught, and she confronted a herd of well-established professors at the university, all male. She was in the fight alone, verbally, and I attended some of the fights. I remember her courage in standing up for her ideas and her beliefs, her confidence about what she believed in, her belief in her work, and the updated ideas she was bringing up against the stale ideas that were there at the university, generation after generation." It was her willingness to stand up to the establishment that made the deepest impression on Zena. "She went through real hard times, people putting all kinds of obstacles in her way, and yes, she was still struggling when I came, but she was hanging in there. She was my image of a powerful, assertive woman, and I liked it. I don't know if I would have felt the same if she had been a man. I'm sure I would have appreciated and admired the ideas, but it was expected that a man be powerful;

this woman was powerful when it wasn't expected. And I think this had a bigger influence on me." Their relationship was more than merely refreshing, Zena said; it was transforming. It not only gave her a model for what she wanted to be but also enabled her to believe that she could live the way she wanted to live and do the things she wanted to do despite the resistance she would surely encounter in challenging the status quo.

Many of us grow up believing that heroes must accomplish their goals by relying solely upon their own wits. These beliefs derive from the plethora of stories about male heroes that extol their isolation and independence, promoting the ideas that the true hero needs no help and that the expression of any such need diminishes his heroic stature. But a careful reading of these tales reveals that heroes are aided by allies at critical junctures all along the way and that without such help their quests could not possibly succeed, regardless of their gender.

It is impossible to overestimate the fear, uncertainty, and disorientation felt by fledgling heroes at every stage of the journey, and most would neither undertake nor complete their quests were it not for allies. Allies are forces and guides that intervene at pivotal points to reinforce, encourage, and empower the quester, to help her move from where she is to where she wants to be. They are essential ingredients in the quest motif, the glue that often holds a quester's spirit and vision intact when she is in the throes of awakening or initiation, the spark that attends her transformation, illuminating new pathways for adventure and self-expression.

Allies take a variety of shapes and serve the quester in a variety of ways depending upon which stage of the journey she is traversing. Most frequently they are found among other people. A teacher, therapist, partner, friend, parent, even a literary or historical figure can provide the guidance and validation urgently needed by a quester, whether she is being awakened, initiated, or transformed. Allies come cloaked in the garb of inner experience as well; dreams, intuitions, and paranormal or spiritual events may seem unusual allies to some, but they are not uncommon. During a solitary trip to the ocean, Debra recalled, she was walking down the beach "lamenting my failure to find a relationship and wallowing in self-pity, when I heard a voice—like no voice I knew (and there was nobody talking)—saying, 'Oh, get off it, let it go. When you stop whimpering you'll get exactly what you want.' So I did, and that's just about what happened." As this experience suggests, allies can be quite dramatic, appearing in a form and at a time least expected. But others are so subtle that their presence is detected only when a woman culls her memories for evidence of their existence. Occasionally even the most pernicious "dragon" will be seen, in retrospect, as a most influential and essential ally.

Regardless of the form it takes, an ally's purpose is to guide, support, motivate, and strengthen the quester during the rigors of her journey. It "always urges the hero to take risks, to be fully alive . . . to avoid those who tell her to stifle her energy, passion, and individuality, [and to] recognize the heroic opportunity obscured by the apparent catastrophe."[1] It exhorts her to persevere, to refuse to give up or victimize herself, and to remember that "she is worthwhile, that she has a right to happiness and fulfillment, and that she has the ability to find it."[2] Further, it reminds her that she alone has the power to create herself and her life anew no matter how long that process takes.

HARBINGERS OF HOPE

The kind of help an ally provides will depend upon the specific tasks a quester has set for herself and the stage of the journey through which she is passing. In the predawn hours of a quest, before a woman has even begun to realize such an adventure might await her, allies often function as precursors. These guides plant a seed of hope and possibility that will germinate when time, circumstances, and a woman's own determination and inner strength enable her to begin her quest in earnest. They help the budding hero keep alive her spirit, her individuality, and her innermost hopes and dreams, especially if she finds herself in difficult or adverse circumstances. They build a psychological bridge for her to walk across when she feels strong enough to accept the challenge of awakening and to leave her old life behind.

In many women's early lives precursors appear in

the guise of teachers. I remember one such person from my own adolescence. When I was fourteen I entered a progressive high school, an all-female, Catholic school that took seriously its commitment to educate young women to their fullest potential. During my freshman year I had a memorable connection with the instructor who taught philosophy and religion, required courses at our school. For some years prior to that encounter I had been questioning the teachings of the church in which I was raised. I had always been interested in spiritual ideas, but midway through my freshman year I knew I no longer believed nor could practice the tenets of Catholicism; try as I might, they made no sense to me, and I was not very good at pretending that they did. This, of course, threw me into a terrible quandary. I loved my school; it was the only refuge I had from the deep unhappiness of my home, and I did not wish to leave. But because it was a religious institution we were expected to study the Catholic faith and regularly attend religious services, activities I could no longer force myself to do.

After class one afternoon I approached my instructor, Sister Marcelline, and haltingly confided my dilemma, fully expecting to be sent to the principal's office, suspended, and perhaps even expelled. She looked at me with her deep and penetrating eyes, listening with a compassion and respect I was unaccustomed to receiving from adults. When she spoke it was not to send me away in anger or disgrace; instead, she said simply and quietly in her soft Irish brogue, "You cannot give up the quest just because this isn't the way." For the next three years she introduced me to comparative religion and world philosophies while formally excusing my attendance at religious services. She insisted only that I continue to explore the spiritual realm until I found answers I could live with, even if they led into unknown or unfamiliar territory. Without my knowing it at the time, she had become my first ally, her tutorials fortifying me for many trials that lay ahead. I never saw her again after I graduated from high school, but her words and her presence were embedded in my consciousness and are alive to this day, some twenty years later.

Melia also remembered a teacher who was singularly important in her life. When she was fourteen she became very attached to one of her high school teachers, coincidentally also a nun, the first person, she said, who saw value in her refusal to conform to cultural expectations. Every Saturday she would accompany her teacher to the slum sections of their city, helping her distribute clothing among the poor and listening to her give religious instruction to those who requested it. During those years she read widely from the lives of women saints, many of whom she used as role models. "This was not because I loved being a martyr, but I liked their strength, their determination, that they set out to do something and they did it," Melia said. "And it's too bad they got killed, but that wasn't the important part. It was the strength I felt when I was reading their lives."

That vitality was present in her teacher as well. "She was such a strong force, so very important in my life until I was sixteen. For a time I thought I too would be a nun. I'm so glad she told me no, I was too young." She laughed, thinking of her husband and three sons. "But that's the first time someone saw something positive in who I was and how I was behaving. *Rebelliousness* was what they labelled my behavior. Of course I was not being rebellious, I was being assertive. But I was labelled rebellious, and she was the first to see that speaking my mind was something good. Later, when I went to college in the Philippines, another nun took me in. And, again, I bonded with anybody in my country who did not think badly of my assertiveness. Because this is a different trait. People really didn't like this about me, even my own family. Not the school system, not even college. But one nun said it's okay to be assertive. So I was."

Precursor allies encourage us to explore our deepest values and discover our inner resources, largely by believing in our capacity to comprehend and grow from our experience. They reach out to listen and to guide us as we take our first tentative steps in the direction of our quest; by having faith in the integrity of our thoughts and feelings, they teach us to have faith in ourselves. A sixth-grade English teacher who was aware of the turmoil in Leah's family allowed her to talk for hours on end, challenged her intellectually, and refused to let her take the easy way out of any assignment, a discipline that would stand her in good stead in the coming years. Another English teacher during her eighth and ninth grades told her repeatedly that she was good, that she could write, and recommended various courses that would improve her command of the language. "She mentored me and taught me grammar and would be horrified to hear me saying 'mentored,' " Leah laughed. "She told me to take Latin to understand English better, so I did. Anything she said to do I would have done, because she had a lot of faith in me." A Hebrew teacher with whom Leah spent a year and a half preparing for her bat mitzvah taught her to appreciate the poetry of the Hebrew language in a way she never had before and kept her connected to her Jewishness at a time when many adolescents break away from the faith into which they were born. This too would serve as an important source of strength for Leah as she grew older.

When a woman is caught in the throes or the aftermath of an abusive or dysfunctional home, precursor allies often act as surrogate parents, helping to keep the woman physically and emotionally alive. "Mrs. Hotchkiss was the person with whom my mother sent me off to Sunday school in the Christian Science Church when I was five," Eileen remembered. "My mother had no room in the drudgery of her life for church, nor did she ever send my brothers; I continue to wonder why she sent me. Today I know nothing about that church, but I suspect that Mrs. Hotchkiss shaped me into a deeply spiritual person of a deep faith, if not a religious person. She saw to it that I had nice clothes for church and took me on my own great shopping events. But most of all she did it by loving me and giving me back my best self."

As a lonely and sensitive child struggling to cope with her mother's mental illness and her father's alcoholism, Sarah was deeply affected by the absence of love and nurturing in her family. "But somehow I realized where the deficits were within my own life, or within my parenting, and I sought out people who could fill those gaps. I went looking for substitutes. Some of my friends' parents were willing to teach me things like baking cookies or doing the hula hoop, but one in particular took a special interest in me. She was one of the neighbor kids' moms, a wonderful person whom I took on as a surrogate mom. My surrogate mom sort of took over when my parents split up and my stepmother wasn't in the house and I was there with my father and my sister. She'd come and take care of us. We'd go over and watch her make bread and those kinds of things." What this ally did was far less important to Sarah than the quality and availability of her emotional presence, without which, Sarah felt, she would have lost herself in an abyss of depression and despair.

Leah remembered a similar ally in Larry, a man who helped her stay physically alive during the years that preceded the first of her awakening experiences. "Larry managed a coffeehouse, and he had known me since I was in high school because I used to sing at open-mike nights at a place called 'La Cave.' He remembered me in part because my mother picked me up, brought me there, and sat in the back looking suspicious. I didn't drive until I was past twenty, so someone had to take me there. It was in a bad neighborhood. And Larry was somebody who, at a time when I was going to go off and kill myself, literally, physically caught me and stopped me. And was always there during those years of my adolescence, cheering for me, making sure that I was safe, performing a parental function of sorts. There weren't a lot of 'good' grown-ups in my life. There were lots of adults, but he was the kind who made sure that I was off the street at night and doing something that felt good. In an odd sort of way he kept me from being isolated, helped me to be more of a social human being, which I was not and probably never will be. But he kept me from dying of my isolation."

It is important to realize that the length of time any ally is present in a woman's life can be completely unrelated to the power and duration of its influence. When Annie was fifteen she was required to participate in a physical education class that she loathed, led by a dance and exercise instructor whom she adored. One day her teacher invited her for coffee after school, and they sat and talked for about an hour and a half. "I can't even remember her name," Annie said. "We never went out again, but I still remember the incredible feeling I had sitting there with her. She helped me know that I would grow up someday, that I would get to become a whole adult person, that there would be lots more pieces to me that I didn't yet have. And I realized that she didn't think less of me—or the person I would become—because I was rotten at dance and exercise. She taught me that it was okay to be better or worse at various things but that didn't make me less of a person. And I never forgot that."

Furthermore, allies need not be physically present for their help to reach a quester's consciousness. Pam had been sexually abused by several members of her family for many years, a highly traumatic situation compounded by the isolation of her youth and adolescence and her lack of friends or mentors. Yet she was able to endure until she was old enough to leave home by looking to "myself and what I'd seen from afar of the black mothers of my schoolmates living in the South in the 1960s." Somehow, she felt, if they could survive, then so could she. Pam's experience illustrates how allies can be recognized and drawn upon regardless of whether they are physically present or even aware of their role in a quester's life. No matter how lonely or isolated a woman might feel, no matter what her age or how dire her circumstances, there is always some source of guidance in her environment that can stimulate the development of her courage, stamina, ingenuity, and will and prepare her psychologically for the coming journey. The budding quester, however, must be willing to reach toward and act upon help whenever and wherever it is to be found. No matter how powerful an ally might be, it cannot take that initial, crucial leap of faith for her; the quester must do that alone.

ALLIES OF AWAKENING

Once a woman is called to awaken, her need for an ally becomes especially acute. As seen in chapter 2, an awakening will change a woman's life in some fundamental way, occasionally as the result of conscious volition but often through circumstances seemingly beyond her control. A relationship begins or ends; a career path veers in an unexpected direction or comes to an abrupt halt; previously held beliefs or values suddenly shatter; physical or emotional health collapses; unexpressed memories or parts of herself rise from the depths of her innermost being and demand to be recognized and integrated. Whatever the form of its outward manifestation, an awakening always calls the quester to emerge from the chrysalis of her former life and risk becoming a more fully functioning human being.

A primary purpose of an ally during this time is to help the quester acknowledge the reality of what is transpiring and encourage her to accept the challenge of awakening. When Joan was deciding whether to take the "road less travelled" and enter religious life, her father supported her decision even though he was not a member of the church to which she had converted. "He was just a very caring person, a helper for everybody. He was a person who deeply loved. When I decided to enter the order and go away, it was he who encouraged me to go, who told me to try, whatever happens. He said to know that I always could come home, but to give it a try." Carolyn, a single parent with three young children, found herself shaking her five-year-old daughter one morning to get her out the door and off to school. Frightened by the realization that she was acting out her own frustrations and inadequate coping skills, she entered therapy only to find herself mistreated and misled by her counselor. Carolyn ended that relationships and took the enormous risk of beginning another therapeutic partnership. This time she found a psychologist who taught her "the gentle power of self-love" and helped her discover her history, her needs, and, she emphasized, her strengths.

There is often a sense of disbelief about awakenings, a feeling that whatever is happening could not possibly be happening. This feeling is present whether a woman is uncovering memories of physical, emotional, or sexual abuse; acknowledging the presence of an addiction in herself or in a significant other; dealing with death, divorce, or separation; or bringing to a close a familiar way of life. As the quester parts the veils that block her vision, allies validate the reality of her new perceptions. Like genies in ancient Arabian tales, they reveal the existence of hidden doors to possible future selves. Although no one but the quester can unlock those doors, allies show her where to find and how to use the key. They relax her grip on outworn images of herself, nudge her from ruts she may be frightened or reluctant to leave, and guide her as she takes her first steps in a new direction.

Such an ally came into Leah's life when she was

nineteen and deciding whether to come out as a lesbian. "She was the first person who ever said the word *lesbian* around me and the first woman I ever fell in love with. She was an amazing person, a real sixties hippie, sort of like a sprite. She was a marvelous human being. She helped keep me free of a lot of my preconceptions, she loosened me up. And she was willing to live on the edge all the time. I'm this very stodgy person in a lot of ways," Leah laughed, "a good Capricorn, very rooted and predictable. I take the prudent course most of the time. And she helped loosen me up because to come out, even though it felt right, was also terribly frightening. So she was really important in mentoring me through that transition."

Susan's husband recognized her intelligence and potential long before she was able to do so herself. Several years ago he signed her up for a conference for and about highly capable women and insisted that she belonged there. That experience proved catalytic, propelling her into reexamining her life options and reshaping her career goals, and eventually freeing her from old and debilitating beliefs about herself.

Mary, a communications specialist in her early forties, discussed two women who played pivotal, albeit bit parts earlier in her life. "One was a placement counselor who looked at my new B.A. and my resume and told me I had a great future in kitchen work. That made me angry and motivated me to get off my duff. The second was a guidance counselor I saw while trying to put together a postgraduate study program. It looked like the rules of the bureaucracy made it impossible to do what I wanted to do. And she told me that nothing was impossible, that I could do anything I wanted if I took the time to figure out how to do it properly. She gave me hope."

When I think back to my decision to leave the East Coast and start a new life on the other side of the continent, I often wonder whether I would or could have taken that risk had it not been for a very brief encounter with a dentist I saw for only one consultation. The stress of deciding whether to leave had taken its toll on my teeth, leaving me with sore and bleeding gums. I made an appointment at a university clinic and settled back for the examination, trying to conceal the tears that were omnipresent during those difficult days. Halfway through his examination this unanticipated ally stopped, sat back, and asked with great kindness whether I was experiencing an unusual amount of stress. In response I immediately began to cry. He placed his hand on my shoulder and said that though he didn't know me, he did know that we were all much stronger than we thought we were and that every problem had a solution, however hopeless that problem might appear. When I complained that I could not possibly undertake the audacious move I was contemplating, he looked at me for a minute or two and then said very firmly, "If you really want to go you'll find a way. If this is really important nothing will stop you unless you let it." What I remember from that encounter was not so much what he said but his willingness to reach out with compassion, encouragement, and faith in my ability to find my way. I left his office feeling a powerful sense of renewed determination and immediately set about planning my move.

It is the rare person who does not lose heart in the face of an awakening, who fails to perceive, at least for a time, the inner resources we each have at our command. Inertia and self-doubt, in conjunction with the mundane and repetitious habits of daily life, all too easily blind us to the totality of who we are and threaten to derail a quester at the very edge of her journey. In such times allies can be mirrors, reflecting back to us the strengths and assets that are hidden in the turmoil of the moment. Every time Melia is faced with a new set of challenges she feels paralyzed by what she perceives to be her intellectual shortcomings. Fortunately one of her former professors always told her she was smart and capable even when she didn't feel that way, a message Melia has internalized and learned to rely upon whenever her belief in herself falters. "Over the years Lisa must have met hundreds of students who were intelligent," she said. "So for her to say that to me, I have to believe it, because she has no reason to play up to me. She always says the same thing. And I hang on to that feedback as something true."

Allies tell us "yes you can" when we say "no I can't." They may offer their shoulders to cry upon when we need comfort and reassurance, but they also know that comfort alone will not empower a woman to withstand the pressures of a quest. Thus they also function as psychological "sherpas," guiding us as we move from somnolence to awakening, exhorting us to take risks we might otherwise forgo. When Sarah met her future husband and for many years thereafter, she felt incapable of living an autonomous life. Her marriage provided the emotional stability she needed in order to leave home and experiment with new ways of being. "I don't like acknowledging that I got into a relationship in order to tag along with somebody who was going places, but the truth is that I went places because of my relationship with my husband. We did some travelling, and I got to see different parts of the country, but I don't think I would have left home had it not been for him. I think I would have found a job close to home, and I'm not sure what my life would have been like, but it would have been very different."

Sarah's husband provided not only a stable emotional base but a role model for actualizing her unrecognized possibilities. His interest in social service sparked her own, propelling her onto a career path she would not otherwise have considered, one that allowed her to reopen inner doors that had been tightly shut for years. She learned to "acknowledge what was inside that was hurting so badly, to think as well as feel what was going on." Over time these lessons enabled her to become more whole than she ever anticipated. They also taught her the impossibility of living life in someone else's shadow.

As Sarah grew stronger her marriage grew weaker, no longer a place of safety from which to explore new horizons but a prison that threatened to suffocate the self that was emerging. "Perhaps going to graduate school and working beyond that point gave me some sense that I could be doing things on my own. I'm not sure. But I was very unhappy in my marriage for a long time. It was important for me to be nurtured, something I didn't feel from my husband. Our relationship dragged on for many years longer than it should have, but I felt I needed some catalyst to help me leave it."

When Sarah finally decided to leave this relationship a new ally appeared who led her to the next stage of her journey. "The person with whom I became involved was a woman. She was extremely nurturing, which was good for me. Because of the life I had led with my parents I had to close down and not show my feelings or even what I was thinking. And so for someone to draw me out in ways that were different from the ways I had used was very important. She was very important. It's interesting that I have chosen people to get me where I have wanted to be, who helped me make the decision I might not have been able to make alone."

There are certainly times in every woman's life when allies seem nowhere in sight, but that does not mean they are unavailable. During the summer after she graduated from high school, Brenda made "the momentous decision to choose college instead of marrying my boyfriend and staying in our small town. I am not sure of the rational process that occurred, but I do recall the sense of enticement and allure that education held for me despite my terror of going off on my own because

I was very shy. I saw college as my escape from an oppressive, anti-intellectual home and town, but I had minimal self-confidence and little sense of direction. Leaving home turned out to change my life forever. It saved my sanity, gave me a future and an identity." In thinking back upon that experience Brenda regretted that no one had been there to help her with it. "I didn't know anyone to consult, and I really wouldn't have known what help I needed." But she was able to awaken herself by drawing upon her own inner allies: her ability to perceive a larger context for her life, her willingness to allow her intuition to direct her toward an unfamiliar path, and her determination to undertake a challenging adventure despite trepidation. A woman's own "larger" self, an enigmatic but formidable ally, is always with her. Accessed through dreams, intuition, attention to her own unconscious process, and an unswerving commitment to growth and self-discovery, it reaches out at every turn to grasp her hand and lead her toward a more authentic life.

ALLIES OF INITIATION

During the awakening allies serve the quester by acknowledging and supporting the reality of her experience, illuminating paths to possible futures, and helping her uncover her inner reservoir of strength and capability. As her relationship to herself deepens and unfolds through the trials of initiation, new allies will appear.

Although allies may continue to serve her, their principal mission is to facilitate her transformation. They do this by deterring her from giving up or getting lost.

The initiation is a period of purification in which the hero's personal past is dissolved, transcended, or transmuted. During the second stage of the heroic journey the quester will encounter a series of dragons that test the limits of her psychological, physical, and spiritual endurance. Whether she is living through the dark night of the soul or freeing herself from intrapsychic, interpersonal, or sociocultural constraints, her transition from awakening to transformation requires that she accomplish three very important tasks. First, she must make her way in the world of men while keeping her own shape; that is, she must define and express her most authentic self in every facet of her life. Second, she must take control of her life, assume responsibility for creating her own future, and refuse to victimize herself in any way. Third, she must accept her own power and learn to trust her own inner strength as the only source on which she can ultimately rely. Awakening is essential but never enough. The quester must consciously and deliberately stay awake, and the allies of initiation will help her to do this.

When Joan entered the convent she was placed in the care of an ally named Helen who would accompany her for the next forty years. "The person who touched my life as a real mentor and who always seemed to be there was a woman who was actually my initial contact when I became a Sister. She was what we would call the

Postulate Mistress. She was the person who instructed us and guided our first months in religious life. Later on she became a province director for a group of Sisters, and I was in her province. And then she became a mother general in this congregation at the time of the big change in the Church in the early 1960s. She was a very influential woman in the life of the sisterhood because she was one of the first women leaders of all the women religious in this country and at the cutting edge of change."

I asked Joan what it was that had made Helen such an invaluable ally. "It was not the positions of increasing responsibility that she occupied," she said, "but the fact that she was a very good friend to me. She had great understanding and was a real human being. She didn't fit any kind of stereotype about Sisters or nuns or religious life because she had such depth of humanness about her and an enormous capacity for caring. She died last February when she was ninety years old. And throughout the crisis times of my religious life when I was considering whether to stay or leave, Helen was there and extremely supportive. She would talk of her own struggles, of her own growing up. Her wisdom was always practical; there were never any platitudes. She never said, 'Well, Sister, if you pray, everything will be alright,' or 'If you just hold on and read a book or get very deeply involved in ministry it'll all go away.' She could recognize and give credibility to any problem, including the struggle of sexuality.

"What made Helen such an invaluable mentor was

her vulnerability. The religious world saw her as this extremely effective leader at a time of great change, chaos, and confusion in our life. There were factions and possible divisions in the communities, but she had the kind of resiliency, strength, and wisdom to build bridges and prevent breaks. But underneath this strong exterior was a very vulnerable and caring human being. When I was hospitalized for five weeks on a psychiatric ward getting over burnout, I didn't want anyone to know. But Helen found out, and she called. She was in her eighties at that time. She was very concerned, interested, and helpful; she gave me complete empathy, understanding, and love. Had Helen not been such a key person I think I would never have been able to get over being frustrated and humiliated at where I was. She reached in. She only wanted me to be where I was at the time. Not to try and move out of that too fast. Not to try to cover it up, not to make excuses for it. Not to ignore it, but to acknowledge the reality of where I was."

The path of initiation leads each of us through periods of dense, unpredictable, and unfathomable wilderness. It follows a winding and arduous trail, full of unexpected obstacles and startling twists of fate. Because each of our paths is unique there are few signposts to mark the way, and thus it is very easy to become lost or disoriented. There are times when a seemingly well-marked track will disappear into thick underbrush, obliterating all signs that it ever existed. Sometimes a fork will appear in the road, requiring a quester to choose between equally obscure possibilities. Occasionally an enormous and unforeseen obstacle will loom large on the horizon, forcing her to confront it directly or forge a new trail to detour around it. The psychological climate of a quest can suddenly shift from relative calm to fearsome storm, leaving a woman loath to venture further for fear of what might befall her. All paths have their perils and pitfalls. Every quester runs the risk of depleting her stores of physical, psychological, or spiritual energy before her journey is completed. No quester can win her way through to transformation without the timely intervention of her allies.

These guides have an uncanny way of appearing, illuminating choices we might otherwise have rejected, offering nourishment we might otherwise have refused. Annie shook her head and laughed when she found herself describing her cousin Randy as a guiding force in her own life. Randy was a year older than Annie and not someone about whom she felt particularly fond. "When we would come home from school I would get a glass of skim milk and half a cookie, while she could eat baked potatoes and drink chocolate milkshakes. Randy wasn't very bright. But she has been a tremendous influence on my life because since she was a year older than I was, she always was an example for me to follow. She happened to get married the year before I did. She had children before I did. And whenever there was something that I was worried about doing, my internal response was, if my damn cousin Randy can do this, I can do this. And that's how I had babies. And that's how I did all sorts of things that were very scary for me. Now that's a strange kind of influence, but it was an influence."

I too encountered an unusual ally when I hitch-hiked out of Boston in 1972. Although I had no idea where I was going, the decision was made for me during the course of my first ride. A young woman stopped to offer me a lift; she had recently graduated from college and was heading home to the Midwest to decide what to do next in her life. She asked where I was going, and without knowing the answer to her question I sponta-neously replied, "Berkeley, California." She offered to drive me as far as her home, but the more we talked the more entranced she became with the romance of my ad-venture. As we drove through Erie, Pennsylvania, regal-ing each other with stories of our college friends, she recalled that two of hers had recently moved to Berkeley to attend graduate school. Suddenly she turned and looked at me with surprise in her eyes. She was between jobs, she said, and had no immediate plans for the fu-ture. Why didn't she just drive me all the way to Cali fornia and surprise them with a visit?

How could I refuse such an offer? We immediately decided to turn left and explore the southern states on our way to the coast. Our journey across the continent took about two months to complete, a period of time punctuated with moments of hilarity and exhilaration as well as anxiety and fear. But the farther west we trav-elled, the more uncertain I became. Somewhere in the Arizona desert, after a narrowly averted and potentially fatal car accident, I had the first of a series of dreams that recurred on three successive nights. In my dream I was travelling through mountains larger than any I had ever seen before, surrounded by endless forests of immense trees; in the distance a snake of bright light glowed in the darkness. Intrigued as I was when it repeated itself, the dream made no sense to me, and I put it away as an interesting but irrelevant experience.

Four days later we arrived in Berkeley, where I planned to spend a few days at the home of her friends while looking for work and a place to live. As I spread my sleeping bag on the floor of their spare room I burst into tears, suddenly and absolutely certain that my journey was not at an end, that this was not the area in which I would resettle myself. But I had barely one dollar left in my pocket and no idea what to do next. When I awoke the next morning I had a distinct impression that I should take a bus into San Francisco, a short trip that would nonetheless deplete my meager funds. The intuition was insistent, so I dressed and departed. Some time later, as the bus pulled up in front of a downtown terminal, my inner voice told me to disembark, and I complied. I walked through the main doors and literally into an old friend from the east whom I had not seen for many years, sitting on top of his luggage. After recovering from the shock of rediscovery, we sat in a cafe drinking coffee and telling our stories; he, it seemed, had been vacationing in the Bay Area for the weekend and was about to return to his home in the Pacific Northwest. After listening to the story of my odyssey he asked if I would like to accompany him north;

he would pay my train fare and house me until I was able to get back on my feet and determine my next move. Having no other option, I agreed, though not without considerable trepidation.

Later that evening we settled ourselves into our Amtrak seats and I promptly fell asleep, emotionally spent by the day's astonishing turn of events. Sometime during the early-morning hours I suddenly awoke, feeling as if someone were shaking me and calling my name. The car was dimly lit, and everyone else seemed to be asleep. A small inner voice told me to look out the window. As my gaze settled on the darkened landscape I saw with a start that we were somewhere in the mountains of southern Oregon. My dream "snake of light" was the train curling through the passes, its headlight illuminating huge trees indigenous to the region. I knew then that although I had no idea where I was going, I was at least headed in the right direction.

Allies give us many gifts. Sometimes they feed us cookies and milk or lend us the fare to a new destination. Sometimes they teach us how to pace ourselves, how to intersperse play and recreation with the hard work of growth and self-discovery. Sometimes they listen as we sort through the experiences of our lives, separating the wheat from the chaff, helping us make sense of where we have been or are hoping to go. Sometimes they teach us to stay with ourselves in the here and now, acknowledging the validity of choices we made even if, in retrospect, they seem not to have been particularly fortuitous. Sometimes they inspire us with stories of their own struggles, being models of learning, growth, and self-acceptance, helping us cope with our own set of challenges. Sometimes they force us out of quagmires of self-pity, old patterns, or despair. Sometimes they bolster our visions and dreams when we meet with disapproval or rejection from others. "Sometimes," Kristen said, "when I'm surrounded by people, especially family members, who are leading very different kinds of lives, I wonder if I should be that way instead, or if what I'm doing is really a good thing to do. So during those times I've learned to reach out to people who I've seen or admired and who are doing work similar to my own." By consciously perceiving the value of their work Kristen is able to surmount her self-doubt, fortify her flagging spirits, and reinforce her belief in and respect for the vocation she has chosen.

It is always easier to allow someone into our lives when we feel intellectually, physically, and emotionally strong, but few of us feel that way during an initiation. When our pain is at its most intense, when life presents one crisis after another, when grief, shame, helplessness, or rage leads us to withdraw and isolate ourselves, our need for allies is very real. Those who are willing and able to be there during such times are perhaps our truest friends. They do not talk us out of our pain or diminish the intensity of whatever we are passing through. They do not solve our problems for us. Instead, they walk the passage by our sides, acknowledging our courage and our essential vulnerability as fully human beings, reminding us of our inability to control all the circumstances of our lives, allowing us to make mistakes, teaching us the wisdom of failure, and revitalizing our commitment to our quest by the simple yet powerful gift of their belief in us.

Life would have been unendurably difficult during the years when Melia was having a child every three years and dealing with pregnancy, childbirth, and recovery, had it not been for the support of her mother. "She came from the Philippines every time I had a baby and stayed for a year, to help me with the child care and my postpartum and to help me with my self-image, which has been very hard for me to maintain. I need at least a year of recovery after each baby to get reorganized as an intact person. She stayed with me and always reminded me that I had been able to do it before and would do it again. She always said, 'Regret should not be part of your vocabulary. Regret is only going to happen if you procrastinate. So if you do not procrastinate, you'll do what you have to do. So do it if you think it is right, do it.' And I always remember that. If ever I feel stuck, if ever I procrastinate over big decisions, I always hear her voice saying, 'Do it, or you will be sad. Regret is a sad word.' And I do it, because I hear her voice in the background."

The religious faith in which Annie was raised serves her as a potent source of comfort and guidance during the difficult times of her life. "One of the things that I've always said appealed to me about Judaism is that you could ask as many questions as you wanted to. And I'm a question asker. I truly have a sense that there is an ethical base to this religion that probably isn't terribly different from the ethical bases of lots of religions, except that it's the one I know. And it has to do with fairness and the way you treat other people. I think for me the best symbol of these ethics is the holiday of Yom Kippur, the Day of Atonement and the holiest day of the year, a time when you atone for your sins. But the way it's constructed is that you only ask forgiveness for sins that are committed against God, which would be breaking the Ten Commandments or other commandments that are in the Torah. If you fouled up somehow with another human being, it is your responsibility to straighten that out. You cannot ask for forgiveness from God for that. That's your responsibility. When I was a very little girl, my grandfather used to take me just before Yom Kippur to my friends to see if I had anything that I needed to apologize for or straighten out. This is a custom that observant adults practice. I don't anymore, but it stuck with me. Maybe that's one of the reasons I've always felt so responsible," she laughed. "But there is a wholeness for me in that custom that is real important. It is a religious connection that seems to allow me to use both my intellect and my spirituality or my sense of emotion."

No matter how valuable or necessary allies might be, they are powerless to intervene unless a quester allows herself to ask for help. This is one of the most critical skills a fledgling hero can acquire during her quest. Although the initiation demands that she develop her resourcefulness, resiliency, and self-reliance, it does not

ask her to do this in a vacuum. On the contrary, it challenges her to forgo the limited masculine ideal of
isolated self-sufficiency and permit herself to evolve
and mature within the context of an empowering
community.

Leah recalled a transforming experience she had in
her mid-twenties while participating in a therapy group
as a graduate student. "It was led by this incredible
woman named Emily. I remember sitting there in group
wanting to ask for something. I think I wanted to ask to
be held. I was petrified. And I have this memory that
the room went gray around me like I was dead, because
I was so paralyzed with terror. I couldn't think. I
couldn't move. I couldn't speak. All I could see was
Emily across the room saying, 'You can ask for what
you want. We won't give you what you won't ask for,
but you can ask for what you want.' And me breaking
through this incredible internal thing about asking for
nurturance, and asking. That's when I stopped being a
depressed person, when I learned that I could ask for
someone to take care of me. I'd been so self-sufficient all
my life, and I still am to a great degree, but learning that
I could ask for help was the end of my depression."

In learning to ask for help a quester learns whom,
when, and how much she can trust. She comes to appreciate the delicate balance between asking for help from
others and asking for help from herself, a balance that
constantly changes, a balance that only she can define.
She learns that asking does not always mean receiving
from a particular source. Rather, through a process of

trial and error, she learns to differentiate those people, situations, and impulses that empower her and those that do not. She learns how to use her intelligence and intuition to construct internal boundaries that are solid and enduring yet selectively permeable, that permit her to be open and vulnerable while protected against untoward intrusion. She learns to recognize what she needs in the moment, relying upon her own inner guidance and resources when she can, turning to others for what she cannot give to herself.

I have heard many women express great reluctance about asking for help, believing that to do so might expose them to rejection or humiliation or reenforce their status as weak, ineffectual, and powerless. This, I believe, is a direct legacy of the male model of heroism that dichotomizes independence and relatedness, promotes autonomy at the expense of intimacy and connection, and extols the virtues of stoic isolation while ignoring its very real and debilitating consequences. In my experience, it is *not* asking for help that diminishes a quester. A fledgling hero is as likely to be derailed by the dragon of obdurate self-sufficiency as she is by its counterpart dragon of dependency; not only does isolation cut her off from vital sources of extrinsic guidance and nourishment, it limits the extent to which she can tap into and call forth the resources of her inner self.

Earlier in this chapter I described how several women found allies within themselves when no others appeared in their immediate vicinity. Whereas this often occurs by chance during an awakening, the initiation is another story altogether. By the time a woman reaches transformation, she must learn to turn deliberately to herself and know that whatever the vicissitudes of her life, she will always be there for herself. When Leah became ill several years ago she received a great deal of love and support from her partner, friends, and colleagues, but her passage through this ordeal required that she be her most trusted and constant ally. "I was the person I leaned on the heaviest because I needed me to be willing to try things out, to take the risk to do alternative medicine. Certainly lots of people helped me get well, and lots of friends both here and around the country were incredibly loving. But a lot of it was me, just absolutely determined that this was not going to stop me. I could not accept the verdict that I was stuck."

When Zena was forced to cope with the murder of her brother amidst the stress of completing her education and the terror of threatened deportation, she learned that "there is something powerful inside that says, 'You can do it. You can go through it.' It's probably the same spiritual sense that told me when I was eight years old that I can question. I sometimes look back at this experience and think, how did I think this way? What made me think this way? It isn't something in your environment, although the environment has provided the challenging situation. Nothing in my environment told me, 'Here, go ahead and be a challenger.' This was opposite from everything else that they were teaching us. They were teaching obedience, kindness, and not to question anything, and then there was this force pushing me to challenge things and be different. Now, how does that happen? It isn't something that you can rationally dissect. I don't know what to call it. Maybe this is part of the blue sky. This is probably the part of me that won't let go, that keeps hoping that there is or should be something more."

The greatest gift any ally can give us is the gift of our best selves. Being loved, we learn to love ourselves and risk relating fully, mutually, and equally to others. Being respected, we learn to take seriously our own talents and skills, intelligence and intuition, compassion and empathy, visions and dreams. Being trusted, we learn to reach out, to connect, and to trust our own judgment. Being listened to, we learn to hear our own voices and recognize which parts of us are speaking at any given time. Being challenged, we learn to endure and transcend our own experiences, creating our lives from the inside out. Thus fortified, we win our way through the wilderness of initiation and arrive at the threshold of transformation.

FINDING AND USING ALLIES

Whether allies appear out of thin air or are deliberately invited into our lives, a quester must be psychologically prepared for them to help her. "My parents cheer-led all along," Annie mused. "My grandmother cheer-led all along. I mean, the feeling was that I could do anything, and whatever it was I chose to do, they were there.

There was a therapist who was exceptional although it may have been that I just decided to talk for once in my life. So I certainly had allies. I think the issue was that I didn't know how to use the resources. And that's something I learned very late."

How does a quester choose and use her allies? I think she must first ask herself a very important question: What kind of ally does she need? The answer will depend upon the stage of the quest she is passing through and the tasks upon which she is currently engaged. For example, has she entered a period of growth and learning for which a teacher or adviser would be most appropriate? Is she mostly in need of comfort, support, and encouragement from a good friend? Is she in the process of revising her personal or professional goals or beginning to remember and deal with the legacy of physical, sexual, or emotional abuse? In either case a professional ally, such as a therapist, career counselor, or support group, might be the most appropriate and effective source of assistance.

Sometimes a quester is looking for a source of inspiration to help her embark upon a new quest; if so, books and historical or literary figures can be a wellspring of ideas and encouragement. Leah remembered that Phyllis Chesler's book *Women and Madness*[3] had a profound impact upon her life. "It opened my eyes," she said. "A lot of the things I'm interested in now—women and depression, victimization, sex between client and therapist—all come out of that book. Many of my long-term professional interests started by reading her book.

So to that degree Phyllis was a tremendous mentor to me because reading her book gave me a professional direction that I've stayed with in many ways ever since."

Zena recalled the sense of wonder and excitement she felt while reading about Marie Curie when she was very young. "What I really liked reading about her was that she was a scientist who did wonderful work. I was amazed because a scientist, especially a woman scientist, was portrayed as a regular human being. To read in her story that once she danced all night until her shoes were worn away, I liked that. I liked the whole picture of her. She can be this person who is totally different from the role of other women, doing something different, being a scientist, and still have this nice love life and dance and enjoy her life. And I was jealous of her being so smart and being able to be so fulfilled. But she gave me hope that I could be different too."

By identifying the specific challenge confronting her, a quester can more readily determine the kind of help she will need to meet and overcome it. The most important point to remember in choosing an ally is that the more a woman knows herself, the better able she will be to recognize an ally when one appears.

At the risk of stating the obvious, a quester must recognize that there are different kinds of allies. No one ally can meet all the needs that arise during the course of a quest; rarely is there an "ally for all seasons." The right ally in one situation might well be the wrong ally in the next, either because our circumstances have changed or because an ally can take us no further than she or he has gone. How does a quester know when she has found the right ally? Eileen's words are very apt: "They gave me back to myself each time I got lost." A quester must assess and periodically reexamine an ally's effects upon her intellectual, emotional, and spiritual well-being. Does a particular ally reinforce her sense of competence, self-esteem, and self-worth? Does the quester feel more whole? Does an ally have the necessary credentials or training to help her accomplish a specific set of goals, and are that ally's ethics and values consistent with her own? Just as there are "wolves in sheep's clothing," so can a dragon occasionally masquerade as an ally; asking these questions can help the quester discern one from the other. A quester must also realize that she is likely to outgrow an ally or two (or more) as she evolves over the course of a quest. When this happens she must be willing to let go and move on; otherwise, as Sarah found when she stayed in her first marriage longer than she knew she should, her ally can become a difficult dragon.

What makes for an effective ally? Joan's description of her mentor, Helen, contains a number of qualities that are clearly important: tolerance, openness, integrity, honesty, clarity, and respect, as well as a strong sense of one's own humanity and vulnerability. The position an ally holds in life is important only if a quester is in need of some specific form of "technical assistance" such as from a teacher, therapist, or healer. But it is important to remember that allies are neither perfect nor fully formed; as long as they are still alive they, too, are questers, embarked upon their own journeys even as they render assistance to others. Perhaps the most effective ally of all is the one who knows that.

A quester must keep in mind that it is possible to become overdependent upon an ally, to rely too heavily upon his or her presence. Alliance is an interactive process. A fledgling hero must certainly be able to ask for assistance when she needs it, but not to the extent of compromising or losing her identity or self-reliance. Conversely, as Leah found, it is possible to become self-sufficient to the point of isolation and alienation. No one can operate optimally without allies. Just because a quester may be able to travel alone does not mean that that is the best or wisest course for her to take. Although a rigidly maintained independence may feel very safe, it should be clear by now that safety is not part of the quest motif. The optimal state toward which to strive, I believe, is a fluid interdependence that celebrates the independence and uniqueness of the individual within the context of a supportive and well-functioning community. This may not be an easy state to achieve or maintain, but it is one that increasing numbers of women are recognizing as vital to our survival and the health of our planet.[4]

Finally, a quester must remember that the heroic quest is not a linear process and that allies, like calls to awaken or dragons of initiation, do not show up on any particular schedule. Sometimes an ally will herald a woman's transformation long before she even thinks about waking up. Sometimes she will receive intimations of a new awakening while caught in the throes of an initiation. Sometimes an ally will profoundly change a quester's life without either one recognizing that the other exists. We never know when or where an ally will appear. There are always surprises on the journey; the most amazing and miraculous events can occur. Allies are partners in that intricate, exuberant dance of unfolding, guiding us through passages of awakening and initiation, leading us deeper into ourselves, escorting us to the portal of transformation, and applauding as we leap through, alone.

At the end of a long, challenging, and extremely productive process of therapy, a client of mine shared the following dream. "I dreamt that I took over a small business from you," she said, "and in the beginning everything was in shambles, everything was chaotic. I didn't know anything about running a business, but I knew that if I took a deep breath and went slowly, everything would work out. I would learn. I could do it. And I did."

CHAPTER FIVE

Transformation
and Return

*I*was twenty-five when I suffered a cardiac arrest and clinical death, preceded by a deep depression. In the months leading up to this event I had been engrossed in completing my undergraduate degree and preparing to enter law school and had spent the summer in England studying history with a beloved professor. While there, I had found the time and space to reconnect with myself in a way that had not been possible while struggling to keep body and soul together as a working student. It was also a time-out from the demands of a relationship that wasn't going well but which I wasn't yet prepared to leave. I returned home in early autumn feeling refreshed and invigorated, but shortly thereafter the bottom fell out of my psyche. One morning, while poring over a paper I was writing for a course in constitutional law, I suddenly knew that both my personal life and my vocational plans were headed in the wrong directions.

Since my desperate journey from one coast to the other three years earlier in search of a home, I had slowly rebuilt my life, entering into a full-time relationship and returning to college to prepare for a profession in law. Now both these psychological building blocks were falling apart. My relationship was collapsing under the weight of temperamental and philosophical differences that alienated my partner and me, differences I could no longer ignore or deny. At the same time my values, ethics, and sense of integrity, which had not been consulted when I laid my career plans, now rose in rebellion, refusing to allow me to continue down the path I had chosen. In a blinding flash of insight I knew that I could no more make the compromises inherent in the practice of law than I could breathe underwater without an oxygen tank. The impact of these twin realizations was devastating. My relationship, though fraught with difficulties, had provided the emotional stability I needed to develop intellectually and set my sights on a legal career, the first real goal I had ever set for myself. Together they had enabled me to organize my life in a way that gave it much-needed meaning and direction. Now, in one fell swoop of awareness, that scaffolding was gone. I awoke a few days later, on a blustery morning in October, unaware that I was about to undergo an experience that would transform every aspect of my life.

For many years prior to this event I had been

studying philosophy and metaphysics and practicing yoga and meditation, seeking a context in which to understand my life experiences. During the previous summer while studying abroad I had narrowed my search to three basic questions, the answers to which I had been unable to discern. Was there ever a time when consciousness was annihilated, a time when one's identity was extinguished forever? How did the universe work? Was it a meaningless jumble of haphazard events, or was there really some greater design at play? And what was the point of it all? More specifically, what was the point of my own life? My near-death experience was about to provide some answers to all three.

Sometime in midmorning I realized that my heart was starting to race. My mild curiosity quickly turned to alarm when, instead of lapsing into its normal pace, my heart rate showed no signs of slowing down. I had no idea what was happening to me and, anxious and afraid, I turned to my partner and told him I thought I was having a heart attack. Within seconds I realized I was going to die, though a part of me shrieked, "That's impossible! I'm only twenty-five, I'm too young to die!" I was terrified and unprepared, but there was no turning back. Suddenly a voice pierced through my fear, reminding me of something I had read long ago, that death was our constant companion, always on the left shoulder. The memory caused an abrupt shift in my emotional state, replacing the terror of impending death with the deep calm of acquiescence. I let go and allowed myself to die.

Once I accepted the fact that I was dying I felt a tremendous sense of excitement and relief, and then my heart just stopped. I watched my body fall to the ground, feeling a twinge of sadness that I had not said good-bye to my companion, but the pull to leave was far stronger than the desire to remain. It seemed as if a door that had been there all along had suddenly been thrown wide open, and I turned and raced through it.

I found myself sprinting through the darkened tunnel so many near-death survivors have described, bursting into a level of reality in which everything seemed to be dancing and changing in constant but orderly motion. I entered into this dance, observing and experiencing my "self" combining and recombining in a seemingly infinite number and variety of forms. Some were organic, some inorganic; some were familiar while others were profoundly unfamiliar, at least in human terms. Sometimes I found myself occupying infinitesimally small particulate substances and then rapidly expanding to form a great gestalt. At the height of this experience I realized with a shock that I had no form at all. Yet all the while I continued to exist and to know myself, regardless of the form, or lack thereof, in which I found myself. Amidst the zany exhilaration of this roller-coaster ride through the possibilities of consciousness, I perceived that this experience was designed to answer the first of my three conundrums. There was, it seemed, no point at which I did not know who "I" was; identity was inviolable, unremitting, and illimitable, much to my considerable relief.

With this realization I was whisked back into my body, which my partner, skilled in emergency medical procedures, had carried to our bed and over which he was laboring to apply CPR. Rather than feeling grateful for his ministrations, however, I was angry, upset, and in considerable pain. I did not want to be "back," and I was determined not to stay. I turned around and left again, once more rushing through the passageway I had discovered on my first excursion into the realms of death.

This time I was drawn toward a new and very different level of reality, a large, classroomlike structure in the middle of somewhere, where a professorial-looking being awaited my arrival. As I placed myself beside her she looked at me with empathy and mirth in her eyes and asked me what it was that I wished to know. "I want to know everything," I said, feeling as though I had been waiting a lifetime to say this precise thought to someone who might actually know. "I want to know how it all works." "Is that all?" she laughed. "Then watch."

The ceiling disappeared, becoming instead an enormous blackboard upon which were written long and complex equations which inexplicably made perfect sense. Each symbol contained a vast yet precise amount of information that I was invited to study, touch, and experience at my leisure. Every time I asked my guide for clarification of some concept or point, the symbols would swirl and rearrange themselves, not ceasing until I reached a measure of comprehension. Although most of the particulars are beyond my ability to translate or recall, the essence of this experience remains as clear today as it was sixteen years ago. The vision of the universe I perceived was neither random nor predetermined but rather a vast and intricately organized community in which everything belonged, and into which everything fit with the precision of a Swiss clock. Any change that occurred anywhere in the whole rippled simultaneously throughout its many parts and was immediately absorbed into a seamless harmony, encompassed by a vast and loving intelligence. It seemed as if I stayed in this classroom for a very long time, asking as many questions as I wished, the answers limited only by my ability to formulate questions. At length I could think of no more and sat back, awestruck by the magnificence of the infrastructure I had beheld. My guide smiled, asked if I was satisfied, and when I sighed my assent returned me forthwith to my familiar body in the material world.

Despite what seemed like hours in my out-of-body state, only minutes had elapsed in the physical world. Although my partner strove to keep me alive, I was no more ready to be reinstated in this reality than I had been before. As I opened my eyes and watched him care for me I was overwhelmed with feelings of love and appreciation for our relationship and a deep puzzlement as to why we had come together, given our irreconcilable and rancorous differences. Looking into his eyes I found myself peering down a long corridor of shared lifetimes, and I laughed when I realized that we were very old and committed friends who had come together to "polish" each others' rough edges as only equally strong substances were capable of doing. With this discovery I felt that my life had completed its course. Having no further desire to stay and a longing to return to the peace and expanded awareness I had just encountered, I touched his face and asked him, please, to stop and let me go, a wish with which he reluctantly complied. This final leave-taking was soft and exquisitely gentle, no longer impelled by impatience but rather more like the strains of a slow farewell. My consciousness floated leisurely upward, past the roof of our home, through the trees, hovering for a moment to marvel over the jewel-like park that is the planet Earth. Then with a last and loving look I turned, took wing, and headed home.

After a journey of dizzying speed I found myself in what seemed like the very center of the universe, a multidimensional vortex comprising an infinite number of intact realities all spinning and pulsating simultaneously. This was the only time during my near-death experience that I felt afraid and disoriented, surrounded by an infinity I could not grasp and in which I felt utterly lost, bereft of any sense of belonging to any one place. I was out of my depth, and I knew it. But just when my terror seemed at its height I was suffused with feelings of safety and love and found myself cradled in the "hands" of a vast presence. Looking up I gazed into an eye of incomprehensible awareness out of which flowed a tear of deep compassion for me, conveying not only acceptance but a complete understanding of why I had arrived so precipitously on its doorstep. I had never felt such love in all my life, and I knew, somehow, that I was looking into the heart of the universe and, inexplicably, into the heart of my self.

With this realization I was slowly carried up and into the eye, materializing in the midst of a group of several immense beings. They laughed as I flopped into place, one of them saying gently and with a total lack of judgment in its voice, "We tried to tell you before you left that you were taking on too much, but you never listen to anyone. You're such an impatient soul." With a delicate shake of a gossamer finger another continued, "Fortunately you did what you set out to do, but it was certainly touch and go at times." Ruefully I had to admit they were right, and that perhaps I had finally learned to pace myself. But what, I asked, was going on in our corner of the universe? I couldn't remember, and the state of the planet seemed far worse than anyone could have anticipated. "Watch," they said, and what unfolded before me was an extraordinary lesson in the history of our species.

It seemed as though we, as a collective consciousness, had been engaged in a crucial experiment for a very long time, attempting to synthesize and harmonize two vast and seemingly dichotomous concepts, one akin to what we call power, the other to what we call ethics or morality. Somehow we had selected the metaphor of duality as a core component of our physical experience, a kind of "secret code" that enabled us to work continuously on the problem even when we were unaware of doing so. Although the result of this experiment was not foreordained, I had a strong sense that we would accomplish our goal, not only because we were capable of doing so but because the completion was necessary to a much larger design unfolding in the universal scheme of things. It was an awesome challenge in which everyone had a vital part to play whether she or he was consciously aware of it or not.

All journeys come to an end. As I sat back gazing in wonder at my ancient companions, they asked what I wished to do at this point, remain where I was or return to my physical life. There was no compulsion, no pressure to decide one way or the other, though they were quick to remind me that I had completed the personal goals that had brought me to birth and was free to choose my next adventure in consciousness. As I pondered what I had learned on this journey I realized that my life had indeed been born of a desire for growth, a growth I had determined could be most efficiently accomplished under conditions of adversity and pain. The higher purpose served by this choice was joy, the joy of being in physical reality, the joy of breaking free of old patterns, the joy of discovering inner resources I might never otherwise have cultivated, and the joy of acquiring a quality of self-knowledge I could achieve nowhere else. And I was reminded that we are never truly alone. Not only does there exist an immense network of intelligent and loving allies who sustain and support us as we struggle to grow, but some portion of our larger self always comprehends what we are doing and where we are heading. No matter where we might find ourselves in the vast complexity of the whole, there is always a level of awareness that is old enough and smart enough to understand. And I was shown that each of us, no matter how small or insignificant we might feel, is vital to the whole, to a depth and degree we are wont to forget.

Did I want to stay or go back, they asked again. The choice was mine and mine alone, but I had to decide quickly, since one could be out of the body for only a brief amount of time before it would be too late to return. No words can capture the excruciating difficulty of this decision. I was quite happy wherever I was, deeply at rest and at home, yet I felt a tremendous curiosity and desire to be involved in the momentous changes I perceived were occurring in our sector of the cosmos. I knew that my life would never be the same and that in some ways it might even be more difficult than it had been before. But curiosity overcame my desire for a vacation. Three times I was asked, and three times I affirmed my decision to return, and after the third I was swiftly restored to my body, the doors to that ineffable realm locking irreversibly behind me. I opened my eyes, burst into tears, and promptly fell asleep.

THE PORTAL OF TRANSFORMATION

There comes a moment in each quest cycle when a woman finds herself poised on the brink of transformation. The challenges of her awakening and initiation have prepared her for this moment. By answering her call to awaken the quester has activated her will and made the pivotal decision to embark upon an extraordinary journey of self-discovery. By meeting and mastering the dragons of her particular initiation she has acquired and strengthened the inner muscles she will need to catapult her from the self she has been into the self she is becoming. Now, without fanfare or forewarning, she finds herself ready to effect her transformation.

Like the awakening, the timing of each transformational moment is unpredictable, its impact indelible. But unlike the awakening, which catches a quester unaware and calls her to embark upon a perilous adventure, the transformation has been anticipated and worked toward. Having won her way through the wilderness of her own growth, she arrives at the threshold of transformation, the departure point from one stage of self-development to the next. Gathering her parachute of courage and inner strength around her, she must now let go of her personal past and leap across the chasm of change, a leap that will propel her into a maturity only hinted at during her awakening.

Several years ago I read about a small species of blue crab living in Chesapeake Bay that had to shed its shell completely before it could grow one that fit the larger being it was becoming. Surrendering its protective shell placed the tiny creature in considerable danger; it was completely vulnerable to the vicissitudes of its environment while it underwent the molting process. The alternative, however, was to slowly suffocate until its life force was eventually extinguished. But though the crab had to make its momentous change alone, it was not left unprotected, for as it began to molt another crab would amble over, surround it with powerful legs, and safeguard it from predators while it accomplished its change. Within a short span of time it would grow a more capacious shell and emerge from its shelter, ready to resume life.

Like the blue crab, each quester who wins her way through to the portal of transformation must discard some part of herself in order to create a larger self and give birth to her own possibilities. Whether she releases herself from a pattern that has prevented her from growing up, from an idea that constricts her vision of what she can be, from a relationship that is abusive or too confining for the self that is emerging, or from an addiction that poisons her soul and imprisons her mind, the quester must let go and trust that she will indeed survive the change. The alternative is suffocation and death.

As I learned so forcefully when I allowed myself to die, letting go is nothing short of terrifying because every time we let go of some part of ourselves, we plunge into the unknown. Twice during that experience I was paralyzed with fear, first when I wondered if I would

find anything after death, and later when I rushed head-
long into an infinity that soon dissolved any sense of
who or where I was. For one interminable moment I
was certain I had lost myself forever, and for months
thereafter I wondered how and if I could cope with
what I had experienced.

The outcome of each leap is guaranteed for no
one; as Adrienne Rich wrote, "the door itself/makes no
promises/it is only a door."[1] But I learned there are two
certainties upon which a quester can confidently rely.
When she leaps she will not be unprotected, for no matter what happens she will always be surrounded by that
indomitable ally, her own larger self. And when she
lands, she will alight on the bedrock of her own being.
The process of transformation promises each quester
not only the death of her old self but a psychological
and spiritual rebirth. She will not be the same at the
end of her quest as she was at the beginning, nor will
she ever return to that former self; but if she is successful, her more authentic and mature self will emerge
while her younger self will be outgrown and integrated.
First, however, she must let go.

Timing, that mysterious and idiosyncratic phenomenon, is an indispensable if exasperating ally at this
stage of the quest. Not only does it take a great deal of
courage to effect a transformation, it also takes patience
and trust in one's own process, qualities the initiation
was designed to instill. Although I have never known
anyone to arrive at the portal and not cross over, the
timing of the leap is unique to each woman, and each of

us must wait until some inner, unconscious part of ourselves knows that we're ready. This "incredible shift," as Sarah described her own experience of transformation, will happen, but on its own schedule. Whatever inner work was begun in the awakening must be completed in the final stages of initiation before the transformation can begin, for a precipitous leap would be as chaotic and counterproductive as not leaping at all.

Sometimes a quester accomplishes a transformation with lightning speed as an insight or awareness explodes the facade of her former self, impelling a sudden shift of consciousness. Such was Leah's experience when, during a group therapy session described in chapter 4, she broke through a formidable internal barrier of isolation and self-sufficiency and allowed herself to ask for love, help, and nurturance. After she landed on the other side, her chronic depression evaporated and never recurred.

Annie recalled a similar experience during a recent and "horrible" spring. Her only daughter, a talented and effervescent young woman in her early twenties, contracted a mysterious, degenerative, and excruciatingly painful illness for which she was hospitalized repeatedly over a period of weeks. Three months later Annie's husband suffered a massive heart attack while on sabbatical some fifteen hundred miles away, and for a brief period of time she feared he would not recover. "I changed totally," Annie said, searching for words to describe this event. "I'm not even sure how one articulates that kind of experience because I changed intellectually, spiritually, and emotionally, overnight. I got a sense of the capacity and the potential for loss as well as an acceptance that that was okay. I learned what was meant by those who said that you had to make what you had as rich as you could for as long as you had it."

"I'm a very different person from who I was six months ago," she continued. "I'm more able to play. My inner child got activated when I realized it was necessary to accept and enjoy what was happening in the present. Once things settled down I was able to concentrate on more than what was happening the next second, and I've been able to work in ways that I hadn't been able to before. I've been able to see much more deeply into things than I did before. I have a sense of wholeness that I did not have. The knowledge that there are lots of things you can't cope with or control makes me feel a great deal more able to cope, on an emotional, intellectual, and spiritual level."

Sometimes the transformative process is considerably slower, extending over a longer span of time, and sometimes only in retrospect do we realize what we have done. As I recovered from and absorbed the impact of my excursion into death I slowly let go of the twin supports that had bolstered my life to that point. I gave up my plans for a legal career and suffered through a series of temporary jobs until I conceived a new plan and was accepted into graduate school in counseling psychology nine months later. This field had not been remotely interesting to me prior to my near-death experience, but now it seemed the perfect place to begin to decipher and integrate that extraordinary event. Another year would pass before I developed sufficient support and inner strength to terminate my relationship with my partner and move on to a new life.

Kristen evolved a similar strength as she watched friends develop and die from AIDS. "My life has always gone along fairly smoothly without a lot of ups and downs," she said. "I haven't experienced any great crises or changes in my life. I've had my share of disappointments and problems, but I haven't had anything major happen to me like losing a parent or a sibling, getting involved in drugs, or having to have an abortion. All the life experiences that I see as being huge just haven't happened to me.

"I was always brought up to believe that I was unusual and different," she continued, "and that my whole family was special and unlike other people in a way that has always been scary for my sisters and me. In some ways that belief probably served us well in terms of being able to pursue what we were really interested in, but it has also been very frightening. My sisters and I have a deep fear of loss because we each grew up thinking, 'Well, I'm not like a normal person, so I shouldn't have to deal with all the normal things I'm supposed to deal with.' "

The process of watching AIDS ravage the lives of her friends gave her a much clearer and more realistic understanding of the wholeness of life. "It makes it easier for me to go on," she realized, "because I see that other people can endure loss and that I can too. I can know someone and they can die and I can go on, without being so terribly frightened of all that. That kind of change has been major for me. I've been really scared that something was going to happen to someone I love or to me because everything has gone relatively well for thirty years. You know, it's like, 'Gee, this can't go on for too much longer,' and that's probably true, but just realizing that I can cope with loss when it happens has been a turning point."

Adhering to our own transformational timetables is crucial because more often than not, whatever we feel we can least afford to part with is precisely that which binds us to an outgrown self, and that part can only be dislodged slowly, gently, and with compassion. Such was Joan's experience when she arrived at the portal and found herself hospitalized for exhaustion and burnout. Only gradually could she perceive that the role she had played so well for forty-one years had become a substitute for her real self.

"The person I was had been steeped in the role of 'Sister,' " Joan recalled, "a member of a religious congregation, a woman of 'poverty, chastity, and obedience,' a woman of simple celibacy living in community. I had been schooled in service and was very responsive to being the best possible nun, educator, pastoral associate, administrator, whatever, for more than twenty years. Now I had to ask myself whether I could also be a person. Could I be at ease with who I am? My burnout stripped me down to saying, I'm Joan ____. Who cares whether you're a Roman Catholic Sister? Who cares what you've achieved, what you've done? You are a human being. You are first of all yourself. Now what does that mean? Could I learn to just be myself and integrate that with who I had been? Could I find a balance in my life, could I integrate time for relaxation, for aesthetic appreciation, for skiing or sports, for all the facets of life, in a holistic way? That was the most difficult challenge of all because in religious life your whole person in many ways is subjugated to who you are as a Sister. But my burnout taught me that the other parts of me were significant too."

"You know," she said, gazing out her window into that not so distant past, "that experience really changed me. It slowed down my life, it made me more aware of networking, of people as significant in my life, of how important relationships are. And it made me realize that I'm just a child as far as relationships go, that I have much to learn about the meaning of loving, sharing, caring relationships."

Crossing the threshold of transformation requires not only trust in our inner timing but a deep faith in our underlying strength. This faith derives not from a false assumption of invincibility but from a hard-won belief in our ability to change, the courage to feel whatever fear or pain we have experienced, and the willingness to let go of the past and create ourselves anew. So many life experiences can hold a quester in thrall, causing her to hide from herself and others and to adhere to external demands and expectations rather than the dictates of her own being. But the experience of transformation restores a woman to her native vitality, wholeness, and creativity, sometimes in a most surprising way.

"My first child was born without anesthesia," Melia said, "and there is a stage called transition in which you just think you're going to lose it or die or something. I can still feel that. The pain is so tremendous. I remember feeling like I would snap or just start breaking things, or if I had a gun I would start shooting people because the pain was so intense. I'd never felt that way before. But just when I thought I was snapping from the tremendous pain I switched to floating; I detached from the pain, I dissociated. It was a decision. It's hard to remember when you're in tremendous pain the power you have in just making the decision 'I cannot take this anymore; I have to do something now to survive.'

"This didn't involve the intellect," she was quick to point out. "It involved the ability to make a decision. I could have gone crazy, I don't know, I've never been pushed that far. Viktor Frankl[2] talks about the meaning of existence and survival that he observed in the Nazi concentration camps, about the ability, the power of the mind to transform. And I was able to do this, to change an extremely negative experience into something very spiritual and empowering. I really felt heroic afterward. All my inferiority because I'm a woman left. I could do this, I did this, I gave birth."

Realizing that she could access her will and detach from intense pain was catalytic, enabling Melia to make several major changes in her life. First, she said, she gained a sense of equality with her husband, something she had never felt before. "Really, for the first time ever I felt equal with him. Before, he was the doctor and I was his little nurse. He was the man. Now I was his equal. It was really powerful. I always use that as my model now. I know that everything I'm doing now is difficult, but not like childbirth. Nothing. Everything else is minor to me." With this realization she resolved to bring her life into balance.

Although she had always had considerable intellectual maturity, Melia's emotional development was a different story altogether. "I was still a child when I came to this country. I didn't want to give anything up. I wanted everything, to absorb everything." Although her intensity and singularity of purpose had enabled her to leave the Philippines and achieve many of her professional goals, these traits also had their dark side, leaving her personal life lopsided and in turmoil. The detachment she achieved through childbirth made her aware not only that she had to change but that she could.

"Much of my history up until that time was achieving, achieving, achieving, and meeting my intellectual needs. Interpersonally I don't think I was a very nice person. I was not nasty, but I'm sure I was pretty aggressive and probably stepped on people's toes because I was after achieving and getting. I'm not that way anymore." Over the next several years Melia worked hard to harmonize her intellectual and emotional needs and to balance her career and family, making room in her life to experience both. "I started thinking and looking at the bigger picture. Before then my picture was very narrow and self-oriented, task-oriented, award- and goal-oriented. Before, I could see only the immediate, but it made me unhappy because it was so superficial. So now I am someone who can detach and see the bigger picture, who can let go of little things for the sake of bigger things, who is more farsighted and much more insightful. This is a change I am very happy to have made. I like it so much better than I ever realized I would."

The process of transformation invites us to participate consciously in the creation of our own selves. By consciously stepping into our unknown, by letting go of decisions or expectations that bind us to the past, we free ourselves to create directions and possibilities that cannot otherwise be called into being. Pam's decision to come out as a lesbian not only restored her to a truthful relationship with herself but allowed her to recognize "that I can be in a relationship that respects equality, is not abusive, and doesn't carry the expectation that I be solely responsible for the relationship's success. Realizing that selfishness rather than self-sacrifice is okay and that I can be proud of my accomplishments and vocal about my needs and wants has been a huge transformation for the child/woman who felt her main mission in life was to assist men in their pursuits of success."

When I was gathering stories for this book, Jody wrote a thoughtful and thought-provoking letter in which she said, "I get the feeling that you want a story of a downtrodden female who gets encouragement or enlightenment from someone and becomes the college-educated woman with a $75,000-per-year job." This is far from the case. Transformation signifies many things in a quester's life, but it does not promise that she will attain a particular rung on any particular career ladder, earn a high income, take a vow of poverty, or have all her dreams come true. It demands neither that she adhere to society's prescriptions for achievement and success nor that she try to meet cultural expectations of "true womanhood." It does not bestow a state of perfection, that impossible standard of behavior that insinuates itself into women's lives through one or more "dragons" described in chapter 3, nor does it bring an end to anxiety, loss, uncertainty, or hardship. It does not guarantee that she will triumph over her enemies or reap fabulous rewards in the tradition of many legendary male heroes, nor that she will overcome every adversity that she encounters. Indeed, as Carolyn Heilbrun observed,

> [R]omances, which end when the woman is married at a very young age, are the only stories for women that end with the sense of peace, all passion spent, that we find in the lives of men. I have read many moving lives of women, but they are painful, the price is high, the anxiety is intense, because there is no script to follow, no story portraying how one is to act, let alone any alternative stories.[3]

What, then, is the transformation? For each woman, in her own way and in her own time, transformation marks the end of an accidental life and the beginning of a deliberate life, one that is lived from the inside out. The quester emerges from the wilderness of her initiation with her spirit restored, renewed, and intact. By uncovering her inner strengths and resources and accepting her humanity in all its complexity, mystery, and vulnerability, she frees herself to live in an authentic and courageous way. She commits herself to herself, accepts responsibility for her own life, and learns to live with loss, ambiguity, and change. In doing so she acquires an optimism tempered by experience, and a faith that permits a deeper, more meaningful experience of life. She learns, finally, "not to try to eliminate all suffering and pain, but to affirm life in all its manifestations, and through this affirmation to transform it."[4]

At several points along her healing journey Sarah raged, grieved, accepted, and broke through layers of pain that had paralyzed her for years. "Sometimes that meant letting go of a decision I had made as a child, or allowing myself to feel some feelings I had decided weren't okay to feel. At those points I felt that I truly was a different person, that I had let go of a whole lot of things and was free in a way I had never been before." One such experience involved the decision to have children, a choice she had wanted to make for many years. "My second husband and I talked a lot about it after we got married, although he eventually decided that wasn't something he wanted to do." This precipitated a deep crisis in their relationship, and for a while she wondered whether their marriage would survive. In the midst of the turmoil Sarah enrolled in a course on spiritual healing, during which she became aware of a past life experience in which she had been a mother. "I suddenly realized that it was okay not to have children in this life," she said. "I really believe that in a past life I had children, and that helped me not only to accept the fact that I wasn't going to have children in this life but to feel that that was okay. It was a wonderful awareness to achieve, and I let go of a lot of desires and social expectations as a result of it. I was freed to do other things instead."

When Zena's brother was killed she was devastated, but as she struggled to accept and make sense of this experience she acquired a new kind of strength. "It gave me a sense of my power to go through this loss. I always thought before that if something like this happened, I would die. I didn't die. I thought I'd go insane, but I didn't. And you know, I have more confidence in my intellectual capacity now. I don't know how much more it can take, how far it's going to be able to stretch, but it took that major blow and I emerged. I emerged with an awareness of the power that is within me and an empathy for others who have suffered similar losses. And I emerged with a sense of resignation to the pain of this life. Not acceptance," she averred when I questioned her about this, "but resignation. There is a difference. For me, acceptance means that you accept the bad. Resignation means that you don't accept it, but you live with it. You go on."

If the female hero's quest followed the formula for the classical heroine, a woman would wait at the portal of transformation for someone, something, or some situation to come along and rescue her, whereupon she would live happily ever after. But a heroine who is rescued inevitably disappears from her own story, never to be heard from again. Whatever happened to Rapunzel, to Sleeping Beauty, to the Little Mermaid, or to Cinderella after they fell in love with the princes of their dreams? When I was about eight I stumbled upon a comic book about the life of Cinderella after she was discovered by the prince, rescued from her life of drudgery, married, and elevated to the status of princess. I still remember the disappointment, confusion, and disillusionment I felt when I realized that "happily ever after" meant staying home and taking care of the castle while her husband sallied forth on new adventures.

Over the years, through many trials and even more errors, I have learned that one can never achieve transformation by being rescued. Although such an experience might bring a brief feeling of relief in its wake, it is a poor substitute for a life of adventure, with all the immediacy, uncertainty, and possibility for self-expression that transformation entails. The act of being rescued prevents a woman from engaging heroically in the world of men on her own terms; rather, it causes her spirit to fall back to sleep. And when she awakes she will only have to wend her way through the very wilderness she had thought to escape. Rescue is but another wily dragon, cunning and seductive in its promise of transformation but failing utterly to deliver on its word.

If a woman is to emerge from the heroine's chrysalis, stretch her wings, and fly higher and freer than she ever thought possible, she must refuse the temptation of rescue, leap through the portal of transformation, and arrive at the center of herself. From this remarkable vantage point she gains a new perspective on her own existence. "It was like walking along the path I've always been on," Margie said, "and coming to an outlook where I could *see*—where I'd come from, where I am, and how the path leads to where I still have to go." On the far side of the portal, a quester reclaims the birthright of her own self and discovers that she has been there all along. "We shall not cease from exploration," the poet T. S. Eliot said. "And the end of all exploring/ Will be to arrive where we started/And know the place for the first time."[5]

In the years following my near-death experience I spent a great deal of time sifting through the events of my life and slowly putting myself back together. It was not much fun, but gradually the pieces fell into place. And then one night I had the following dream: I was standing at a construction site watching the dismantling of my former home. Finally only the framework remained, ready for the creation of a new structure. Suddenly the construction supervisor appeared, telling me

that while workers were removing debris from the base-
ment they had discovered the existence of another
room. This room needed to be examined before the re-
modeling could begin, but the door was locked and no
one could get in. As I stood there wondering what to do
I reached deep into my pockets and found my fingers
curling around a small metal key. I knew this would unlock the door, and that I was the only one who could
enter and see what was inside.

This filled me with dread; who knew what awful
things might lurk in that darkness? But enter I must if
I was ever to get on with the task of reconstruction.
With a great effort of will I reached out, opened the
door, and crossed the threshold.

I found myself in a room that was much older
than any part of my former home, pulsating with
power and astonishingly bright. Before me lay a short
flight of stairs that I slowly descended, looking for the
source of this curious illumination. As I reached the
landing I realized that the light was emanating from be-
neath my feet. I looked down and found that I was
standing on luminescent ground, and I saw with a start
that I was standing on myself.

THE RETURN

To complete the quest cycle, one final challenge remains. In classical mythology the hero must reenter the
world with some elixir or gift to help restore society.

"When the hero-quest has been accomplished . . . the adventurer still must return with [her] life-transmuting trophy . . . back into the kingdom of humanity, where the boon may redound to the renewing of the community, the nation, the planet, or the ten thousand worlds."[6] Having crossed the threshold of transformation and embraced her true self, the quester has freed herself from the grip of the heroine's myth: from passivity, self-denial, and the sacrifice of herself to others' expectations. Now she is asked to give something back to the larger community of which she is a member. The experience of transformation has brought her life to a new level of wholeness and integration, but not for herself alone. The gift of herself that she has received is the very gift she must now give back because "the ultimate aim of the heroic quest must be neither release nor ecstasy for oneself but the wisdom and power to serve others."[7]

The return is another awakening, another point of departure replete with all the challenges, joys, and tribulations of every quest. It can take a myriad of forms, but it must evolve from a woman's sense of her own values and purpose in life, and it must reflect the gift she feels genuinely called to make from within. A hero gives because she chooses to, a heroine gives because she is required to; and therein lies a world of difference.

The following stories reflect some of the plans that the women I interviewed have been conceiving or constructing. Although the precision of their dreams varies, their commitment to realizing them does not.

Annie is teaching general curriculum and instruction to teachers-in-training at a small private university and reactivating her involvement in the field of gifted education. "In a sense that is sort of a coming home for me," she said. "I found out many years after the fact that my parents—my father, my natural mother, and, after he remarried, my now mother—spent my childhood going to classes on gifted children and trying to figure out what to do with me. This was not something I was particularly aware of except that I was always sent to very good, small schools. I did the same things with my own children, which is why I originally decided to enter that field. But I feel like I've come full circle in doing that, and have gotten a broader picture, and am ready to go back and dig into it.

"When my husband had a heart attack I had to sit down and figure out what everything was about and what I was doing. I was fortunate in that at the same time I got a one-year appointment at a university that I had wanted very badly. I knew that I would be able to teach for one year, but I really had to sort some things out that I had not sorted out before. One of the things that I have always had a great deal of trouble with is anything that looks like competition. I am not a very competitive person. I get tense when I'm involved with people who rely on politics and social stuff to do what they want to do rather than the work itself. So there was some terror about going into a university situation. Now I happen to be fortunate in that the place where I am seems to be very solidly grounded in ethics and values, not politics. But having to sit down and say, 'Okay, what is it that I want to do?' was a very new experience for me. And what I want to do is what I always thought I wanted to do: teach, write, read, and be around thinking, caring people.

"This takes me right back to where I started," Annie continued. "It's nurturing of a different kind. In my personal life I am known for having a crowd around that needs to be taken care of, in one way or another. I'll always do that because I'm like that. And that's a great deal of what our family life is about. What I have been able to find through my university teaching is a way of nurturing that is much more holistic and allows me to work with the intellectual as well as the emotional content of nurturing.

"This whole experience really fits with this sense I've always had, that the thing I had to do in this world was to be the best person I could be. What I have to look at now is what being the best person means. And that certainly means making a contribution, possibly not in a big way but just in the way I can, and if that's by touching people in a limited way, I'll do it that way."

Kristen, too, thought she should become involved in work that had larger ramifications, and she shifted her focus away from counseling individuals about pregnancy and disease prevention to creating and administering public health programs. As the director of an AIDS education project, she now spends much of her time managing, planning, and evaluating the project's activities. "The bureaucracy is difficult to work with and can make you lose energy," she said, "but I really love the philosophy of the field, the idea that everybody's health matters equally and that our mission in public health is to look at the whole and protect the public's health. We also focus on improving health through the awareness that health status is completely related to economics, social standing, and education, even though traditional medical systems really don't take any of those issues into consideration."

Although moving into AIDS-related work was a natural outgrowth of Kristen's original interests, her current involvement resulted from a conscious decision. "When I started working in the field I saw it as one of any number of issues I could be working on. But now I see it as an extremely important problem that requires a tremendous amount of energy and a certain kind of calm. A lot of people who work for me and with me don't seem to have that; they fly off the handle when things happen. The work is very draining, and I think one of my better skills is the ability to handle a lot of different pressures and stress.

"I've never been interested in the physical or life sciences," Kristen continued. "I've always been fascinated by social science and literature. When I was ten or eleven I read human interest stories as opposed to world event stories, and I've always felt much more concern for domestic than international issues. I've always had a curiosity and commitment to working with people who were different from myself and who had some needs that were clearly not going to get met unless I helped. I've come to think of myself as pretty realistic and not just knee-jerk about helping others. It's not like I have affection for all the downtrodden people of the world; I'm just interested in human nature and human problems.

"This always made me different from my sisters," Kristen continued. "Although both of my parents certainly espoused similar values and generally lived their own lives that way, my sisters are not that way. But I expect this feeling of commitment will always be embedded in the work I do, that if there could be a 'calling,' that would be mine. I still believe we're put here to make some kind of contribution. Some people are doing other things, but public health is probably where I will always be, working in some way that is meaningful, that gives something to someone else who isn't normally going to get it.

"The other thing I feel called to do is to have and raise healthy children, kids who have an emotionally healthy outlook on the world. I get tired of hearing people say things like, 'Oh, don't have children; the world is too awful.' Yes, the world is awful, but I've always felt very strongly that if you're in some sort of position to be able to raise healthy kids, then not only should you do that, but you should really try to think about it as being part of a whole life. It's a very big decision, which I'm having a little trouble making right now with my husband, but it's an important goal that I hope to realize in the not too distant future."

Melia began a group psychotherapy practice several years ago after she gave birth to her third and last child. This work evolved from her firm belief in the power of groups to help people heal. Eventually she plans to return to her homeland and create a form of group psychotherapy that people there can use.

"The third world countries do not have the money to pay for psychological help on an individual basis," she said. "Really, it's only American culture that uses that form of psychotherapy and pays so much money for it. It's a wonderful opportunity, but it's also luxurious, and it fits the culture of privacy here. People in underdeveloped countries group together to talk about whatever is bothering them. In my country this happens after work. Sure, people drink the equivalent of beer, but the purpose of that is social interaction, to unwind and rehash the day's events. Sometime in the next ten years I'd like to go home to the Philippines with several therapists who will volunteer two weeks of their life to train Filipino social workers to run groups. Those social workers will then train fifty more so that group approaches to mental health will become the modality of treatment in a country that is so afraid of one-to-one psychotherapy, and in a culture where groups are the natural, normal setting. I really believe mental illness can be treated effectively this way, not just with medication. It's cheaper than individual psychotherapy, and it uses a format designed to meet the need for human contact, which everybody has. Humans need humans. Humans need to belong. So this way we could meet the human need and the psychological need at the same time."

The overriding sense of vulnerability with which Zena has lived for many years makes it difficult for her to project herself into the future, yet she, too, has what she calls her fantasies. "I won't call them dreams because I really don't know how I'm going to work toward them. I feel that I'd like to do something for people, especially kids, that will bring them hope, which I didn't have, and a life that I didn't have access to. I would probably do this through education, bring them something that makes them believe they can think, they can question, they can discover. I don't know how or if I will ever be able to go back to Lebanon and function there, but I feel a push, a pull from somewhere asking me to contribute something to the world.

"Actually," she said, "I'm teaching a class at the university now that goes well with my fantasy. It is teaching teachers to teach kids how to think. It also fits into one other goal of mine, which is to transmit to people the possibility of knowing by scientific means. I'm not saying that other means of knowing are not as important, but I feel if people were to adopt this way of knowing and use the processes of science, it would eliminate some of the decisions people make based on prejudice, false information, and rumors. It would give people much more ability to think critically and allow them to make rational decisions. I feel it's a worthy way of knowing. I also think it might reduce some of the hatred preached by some dogmas because if you follow dogma and the dogma preaches hate, you adopt the hate with the dogma.

"But I have some healing to do before I can make plans to do more. That sense of meaninglessness keeps coming and saying, 'Why bother? This whole species is not worth it. The world is not worth it. Just play your role the best you can.' But sometimes the vision of the blue sky comes again, and then I feel the need for these kinds of experiences, and I feel that I have something to give. Maybe when I am in a better emotional state I can make it into something more."

Several years ago Sarah left the field of social work, taking a variety of part-time jobs and returning briefly to secretarial work. She realized, in retrospect, that she was reconnecting with her younger self to see whether social work was something she was actively choosing for herself or something she was doing because she fell into it through her first marriage. "That was a midlife crisis for me. I had gotten burned out, so I took a couple of years off to explore other kinds of things, mostly the arts. And I love to travel, so I explored opportunities to learn about other parts of the world. At the end of that time I decided to go back to social work."

By giving herself this hiatus Sarah was able to integrate social work into her life in a very different way. "I decided the part that I was burned out on was doing therapy. I got very involved with other people's problems, and it was too difficult for me to let go of them. So I decided when I went back to the field that I would do administrative work instead. That was a good decision because I like doing it. It has helped me keep a balance, ensuring that I don't get too hooked into other people's pain."

Sarah took a position with a Native American tribe, administering its health care program. "One of the things that I feel is part of my life's work as a social worker is helping people improve their lives, whether that means making personal changes and getting beyond some roadblocks they put up for themselves, increasing their awareness about healthier life-styles, or improving their economic conditions. Working with the tribe is definitely a challenge. There are lots of wonderful things about it, and some challenging ones as well.

"The challenging part is that I have had to work through prejudice against myself as a non–Native American. After being there for six years I was finally accepted by tribal members not only as someone working for the tribe but as part of their community. I don't feel any prejudice directed against me at this point. The really special parts of my job are getting to know the Native American people with whom I work. They have certain characteristics that are quite wonderful. One of those is a sense of humor, a joy in laughing and joking around, qualities that I've worked hard to acquire for myself. I have tended throughout my life to take things very seriously, so it's been important for me to be around people who like to laugh and enjoy their lives. And life is not always wonderful for the people I work with. This position has made me aware that there can be fun and enjoyment in life as well as pain; it has helped me keep a balance in myself."

Leah's decision to become a psychologist enabled her to transform many of her life experiences in ways she would not have been able to had she chosen a different profession. "For one thing, being a psychologist allowed me to understand the family I grew up in, and who and how I am. This forced me to know myself to a degree that I might not otherwise have been required to, were I not a clinician. So, in that regard, it's been tremendously healing to be in the profession I'm in. And it's allowed me to take my politics and make something solid out of it. Being a feminist psychologist, particularly during the last nine or ten years that I've been doing forensic work, has allowed me to put my theory into practice. I have written over fifty articles, and I write a lot from my own experience. For instance, I wrote about the effects of losing my voice, and of the effect of living in the sociological small town that is the lesbian community. Being able to write, teach, do forensic work and therapy as a feminist, as a Jew, lets me put into practice all the things that I've learned and gives me avenues to change the world.

"There is a series of values, Jewish values and feminist values, that are fundamental to me," Leah continued. "I just finished writing a paper on Jewish women in therapy; it's about how my Judaism informs my feminism. There's a concept in Jewish theology—*tikkun olam*, the healing of the world—that is probably at the core of my life's work. I see this work as healing, empowerment, and social change that I do one person at a time, sometimes one classroom at a time. But I believe that when you touch one person the shock waves from that are tremendous. I don't really have a vision of who I'm going to be or how the world will be when I'm not in it anymore, but I have a vision that informs what I do. I believe that what I'm here to do involves the empowerment of those of us who have had our power taken away by unjust means, the healing of those who have been wounded, and the creation of a more just and sane place where people don't get extra credit for being white, male, heterosexual, young, able-bodied, upper middle class, educated, and Christian."

Joan had always wanted to play a significant role within the Roman Catholic Church, one in which she could make a difference, provide leadership, and empower people. This desire was congruent with the evolving mission of her religious order, which asked its members to assume decision-making roles within the Church and be agents of change. Her prominence as an educator and administrator brought her to the attention of the archbishop of her diocese, and after recovering from her burnout she was offered the highest administrative position a woman had yet attained within the diocese.

"It startles me sometimes when I realize where I am and that I got here," Joan said, "and that I'm respected. Every day is a terribly significant challenge." Her new position drew her into an unaccustomed limelight, and she was showered with media attention as well as criticism from both conservative and liberal factions within the Church. Conservatives opposed her appointment because she was seen as a liberal and a feminist who would speak out too forcefully against sexism in the Church. Liberals reproached her for being too conservative, largely because she would not take a public stand on such controversial issues as reproductive choice and the ordination of women. But, she said, in order to be effective she has to be extremely careful. "I take much care to not have a high profile because I can't afford to face the kind of criticism that would take me down. I'm too vulnerable; if my image was tarnished in any way I would not be effective. I struggle with the male dominance in this church. This is a male church, and at this level it is extremely difficult not to see that. But I also bring my own viewpoints to the leadership of this church, and I feel I can do that most effectively in a very low-key, careful way.

"I speak out to the hierarchy about the Church's attitude toward women. I've been a real pusher for justice and peace in the archdiocese, and I can meet with all of the groups within this church and still maintain a sense of being able to relate with all of them. But I do that cautiously. I'm not in a prophet's role. For example, if I spoke out now about being prochoice I would lose any chance I might have to be effective as a change agent. I must do that little by little within the system because there are terrible obstacles for women in leadership roles in this church."

Throughout her career in education and community organization Joan had worked to bring a new vision of partnership into the hierarchical structures in which she found herself. The challenges she faced in doing so were immense: recruiting qualified women into less than welcoming environments, making those environments more open and hospitable, and fighting the patriarchal attitudes and values that were woven into the fabric of the Church. In her current position she has devoted herself to addressing what for her are burning issues: partnership and responsibility. Can she help the Church return to an earlier vision wherein women and men functioned in community, and wherein individuals assumed roles of great responsibility? Can the Church leadership become more responsive to the needs of women and people of color and begin to grapple with the highly controversial social issues that conflict with official Church policy? "Those issues are monumental issues for the nineties," Joan said, her eyes flashing with intensity and concern. "More and more women are writing off the Church, saying they can't stay because it oppresses them. One of the biggest challenges before me is whether I can keep my sensitivity to these issues and be an agent of change without becoming alienated or compromising my principles. I don't know. I pray for wisdom every day."

Despite the awe she feels at having attained a position of influence, she reminds herself constantly that it could disappear tomorrow. "When the leadership changes the new archbishop may not choose me to stay on. I may not be able to stay if his vision of the Church

challenges my values and my integrity. So in my relationships with people I try to be very open, accepting,
and alive because tomorrow I could be gone. It would
be a terrible mistake to assume an arrogance or a belief
that I am more powerful, because I'm not. I'm told all
the time by groups and individuals that I can be influential and effective, but I'm careful to realize that it
could all be gone tomorrow."

Amidst the challenges arrayed before her, one
looms particularly large: how to handle her power to
generate systemic change in the Church. "I've made it to
a place few women have ever come. Now, what does
that mean?" she asked. Even as she reminds the male
leadership of women's oppression within the Church,
she is extremely sensitive to the ways in which she herself could become an oppressor. "That's where I pray I
will not compromise my own integrity by being in this
job. I could use what power I have to subjugate people
for whom I might not have empathy or sensitivity. For
example, I constantly remind myself that gay and lesbian orientation is something that just is, not something
that is chosen. I hadn't had much experience with gay
individuals and groups before coming to this job, but I
think it's possible that I could be blinded to their needs.
My lack of real understanding for the very conservative
element in the Catholic Church today could make me
oppressive toward those who are much more conservative than I am. I could also be oppressive to women
struggling simply for ordination to the priesthood because I don't believe I'm open to that anymore. I just

don't see getting hung up on women's ordination because I don't want women to come into the same kind of system. I want us instead to redefine what we mean by priesthood, Christian community, and Gospel living.

"So those are my real obstacles. Maybe they're pieces of self-awareness that are just beginning to dawn. There is power in my position; maybe wanting that power is what makes me afraid to let go, be real, and risk exposure on the real cutting-edge issues like abortion. So far I've been cautious and certainly not public. That would take a lot of courage, integrity, and self-determination, and I would like to be there."

"Journeys do not always return full circle," Sarah Lawrence Lightfoot wrote, reflecting upon her mother's voyage from her childhood in rural Mississippi in the years preceding the civil rights movement to her adulthood in New York as a pediatrician and child psychiatrist. "Some . . . journeys require deliberate departures from well-worn paths."[8] Such was the case in my own life when I left my home so many years ago to break the cycle of dysfunction that had imprisoned the members of my family for generations. And I left that well-worn path a second time when my near-death experience catapulted me from my "best-laid plans" and thrust me onto a road I've been travelling ever since.

Both of these departures have informed my personal choices and professional activities in ways I never anticipated they would. Most of the loose ends left by my flight from my parents have never been tied up, and I have had to learn to live with a continuing estrangement that defies all my powers of understanding or explication. But like many of the women in this book, my choice of profession has helped me to live more peaceably with that legacy and to transform it in ways I would otherwise have been unable to do.

Life has never been the same since I came back from death; the insights I gained while in that ineffable realm have in many ways made it more difficult to adapt to a culture that doubts such dimensions exist. I spent many of the ensuing years searching for satisfying and meaningful work, years during which I completed my doctoral degree, working all the while in a variety of jobs. I held some part-time research positions and later directed two community-based drug and alcohol programs for teenagers and a school-to-work transition program for handicapped high school seniors, experiences that, while not completely fulfilling, taught me a great deal and certainly paid the rent. I made some mistakes in my choice of relationships, and when my marriage, my home life, and my work collapsed during a terrible six-month period several years ago, so did the spiritual faith I had once thought invincible. This was indeed the darkest night I could ever remember passing through, and for some time I truly thought I would never see daylight again.

Several experiences helped restore my faith and my will to live. In 1984 I discovered my "calling" to understand the obstacles faced by women who chose to pursue their "great possibilities and desires," and I focused my clinical and scholarly work on helping them identify and face down the dragons that inhibited them from doing so. Then I was asked to become the psychologist for a lively group of teenagers who were skipping high school and enrolling in a program of early college entrance, and their energy, idealism, zany humor, and boundless enthusiasm for life worked their magic and reactivated my own. But it wasn't until I conceived this book and began to see our lives from the larger perspective I had glimpsed so long ago that I came full circle and fully back to life. This book is the gift of that return, for it is my deepest hope that if more women risk becoming the heroes of their own lives, we can indeed transform the world.

CHAPTER SIX

Toward a
New Mythology
of Heroism

O ne evening I sat in the midst of a large and diverse group of women who had gathered to
discuss Susan Faludi's powerful book, *Backlash: The Undeclared War Against American Women*. We
were shocked and appalled by what we had read, though
hardly surprised. We all knew intimately the depth and
magnitude of the "backlash," having felt its devastating
effects in our own and others' lives. And so we sat and
told our stories well into the evening until a silence
slowly settled on the room. "Well," someone finally
asked, "what do we do now?"

There is no one answer to this complex question
that was raised by the writer Christine de Pizan in
fourteenth-century France and by countless women in
countless cultures in the years since. But clearly the pre-
vailing myths of sleeping beauties, tragic heroines,
and patient Griseldas will not show us the way, for they,

like the "backlash watchtowers" described by Faludi, serve only "to blind women to their own prodigious strengths."[1]

"Mirror, mirror on the wall, who is the fairest of them all?" This is the question that opens the tale of Snow White, one of Western culture's most enduring heroines; it is the question that forms the core of most quest stories written for women and girls, and it is the question that serves most forcefully to blind us to our strengths. With this query Snow White's stepmother summons the spirit of her magic mirror to reassure her of her beauty and its hold on her husband, the king. But one fateful day she is abruptly informed that her young stepdaughter has unwittingly surpassed her. Poisoned by jealousy, outrage, and fear, she turns on Snow White and sets out forthwith to destroy her.

We have all been tainted by this patriarchal mirror, which for thousands of years has distorted the true face of woman, reflecting only images that are pleasing and acceptable to men. The spirit of the mirror speaks to us as seductively as it did to Snow White's stepmother, bidding us to swallow our strength and our authentic selves, forswear our great possibilities and desires, and sacrifice our connection to the sisterhood of women so that we might be loved. But the reward it promises—a life lived "happily ever after"—is a gilded illusion of glamour and bliss, cloaking the tragic truth that gilt too often turns to lead, poisoning our lives, our relationships, and our self-esteem and leaving a bitter residue of sorrow, anger, and isolation in its wake.

What would happen if Snow White's stepmother smashed the magic mirror, spurned the spirit that resided therein, swore allegiance to her stepdaughter, and set out to envision herself? What would happen if, along her way, she found a new mirror, a new myth, that reflected an image of our heroic selves, seen through our own eyes? And what would happen if she—and we—used that image to consciously, deliberately reshape the world?

I asked each of the women who participated in this project to peer into this mirror and tell me what they saw. The vision that emerged from their collective imagination reflects, I believe, the power and the promise of a fully human being.

THE FEMALE FACE OF HEROISM

To live heroically a woman must belong to herself alone; she must be the center of her own life. She must pursue a wholeness or integrity that is fluid, inclusive, and interconnected and that does not preclude relationships. This permits her "sexuality, creativity—in fact all her activities and achievements—[to] emanate from and express her individuality. Accordingly, self-expression replaces self-denial as the informing principle of the female hero's life."[2]

Although not extolled in traditional myths, the task of being a fully functioning female human being is a formidable and heroic challenge because a female hero must *insist* upon herself, something that most women are neither taught nor encouraged to do. The heroic woman insists that she will be what she wants to be and what she can be. But though the quest challenges her to incorporate many qualities traditionally reserved for men, her quest would fail were she to become a clone of the male hero. Rather, she must fuse the best attributes of femininity and masculinity and so create a new archetype of heroism that speaks to both women and men. This fusion would make her: independent without being alienated; courageous without being contemptuous of the weak; powerful without dominating or exploiting others; rational without suppressing or abandoning feeling and intuition; autonomous within interconnected, interdependent, and equal relationships; nurturing without denying or sacrificing her own needs; and androgynous without compromising the best attributes of her femaleness but affirming the wholeness inherent in all.

A female hero is not a love object in a romance novel like so many heroines of yore, nor is she a second-class hero. Rather, she is a strong, competent, and effective woman whose power derives from her unfolding awareness of the depths of her spirit and her connection to all other beings. She is self-accepting and self-possessed, and she respects her limitations as a fully human being, knowing that perfection is not part of the heroic equation. She is intellectually, emotionally, and spiritually open, and she transcends stereotypical patterns of feeling and thought by learning to see beyond the obvious and ever more deeply into her heart.

A female hero is determined and brave. No matter how frightened she might feel, she knows that she must forge new pathways, explore untrodden ground, and take what risks she can and must to transform herself and the world in which she lives. And so she is willing to look directly into the eyes of life and deal with whatever she finds there, choosing when, whether, and how to respond to the people and events that surround her. She tackles complex problems in a caring and compassionate way and does not shy away from difficult tasks but attempts to accomplish whatever she can despite the obstacles she encounters along the way. She carefully cultivates her optimism and hope, knowing that she cannot overcome every adversity that befalls her but that she can refuse to allow her spirit to be broken. Her courage, confidence, and inner strength derive from her unswerving commitment to her quest for wholeness and from her hard-won knowledge that she is equal to the challenges that are set before her or she would not have answered their call.

A female hero is, above all, a visionary. She takes her life, her toils, and her own dreams seriously, and she strives to make those dreams a reality even if she does not fully succeed. She carefully hones her talents and skills even when they deviate from long-standing tradition, and she uses them in the service of others even though the cost may be high. She evolves a strong sense of integrity and spiritual health which she seeks to imbue in all aspects of her life, and she believes in an ideal or a higher cause from which she garners resilience and faith. She is able to work alone and with others, to lead as well as follow, because the Grail she seeks, though larger than herself, cannot be reached without her. "There will be no true revolution until we are all heroes," Robin Morgan said. "Greatness is simply a way of life and it must become so for everyone."[3]

Throughout the ages, the Grail has been a powerful and mysterious beacon, calling all who will listen to the task of healing a sick and dying world. Though the goal of the quest has always been the same, the Grail has taken a unique form in every culture in which it appeared. For example, it was perceived by poets in ancient India as a radiant jewel, a token of the Light that animates and guides all living creatures.[4] In sixth-century Welsh legends it was described as a magical cauldron that was guarded by a sisterhood of nine priestesses on the Ile de Sein, an island that became the Avalon of Arthurian tales some six hundred years later.[5] For ninth- and tenth-century Celts, the Grail was a sacred stone with miraculous and youth-preserving properties, and a horn of plenty whose spiritual and material resources were never exhausted.[6] Perhaps its most popular depiction comes from twelfth-century Britain, where it was said to have appeared to the knights seated around King Arthur's Round Table as the chalice used by Christ at the Last Supper, embodying manly ideals of virtue, right conduct, and perfection.[7]

But the symbol of the Grail has another and more

ancient meaning. In the Moorish world it emerged as a feminine womb symbol signifying rebirth.[8] This earliest metaphor is far more fitting to the female hero-path, for our quest, should we choose to embrace it, is to heal the ancient rift and restore the fullness of the female to the ongoing creation of the cosmos. "Once you reject the idea of the Fall in the Garden," Joseph Campbell said, "man is not cut off from his source."[9] But more important, once we reject the idea of the Fall of Eve and all that represents, woman is not cut off from her source, and the strength of our spirit is returned to the world.

As more women find our voices and demand to be heard, as we penetrate domains historically reserved for men, we have an unprecedented opportunity to transform our planet with the values and skills we have honed over the centuries: caring, cooperation, community, and connection. This does not mean exchanging a matriarchal for a patriarchal world order, for that would perpetuate an archaic dualism that has served—and will serve—no one well. Nor does it mean abandoning or denigrating men, for we are inseparable companions on the journey through life. Rather, it means awakening to "the depths of our souls and our position in the universe"[10] and revitalizing our world in every sphere—psychological, relational, spiritual, and ecological. It means imbuing the ethic of individuality with an ethic of empathy that recognizes our absolute interconnectedness and responsibility to each other. And it means fusing the best of what we call female with the best of what we call male and so propelling the whole of humanity toward a greater maturity than we have ever known.

Throughout this book I have argued that if a woman rejected the challenge of awakening she would condemn herself to an empty and embittered existence. But the call to the quest is more urgent than this. Our institutions are decaying on a planetary scale. Our resources are dwindling, our population is exploding, our environment is disintegrating, and our children are killing each other. The threads of violence, ignorance, and despair are woven so deeply into the fabric of our lives that there is no place left to run or hide. We can bemoan this fate, acquiesce to the status quo, and wait for a rescue that will never come, or we can open our eyes and realize that the tools of transformation are in our own hands.

In analyzing population statistics from the U.S. Census Bureau and other sources, Susan Faludi reported that

> Women of the '80s were the majority in the general population, the college campuses, the voting booths, the bookstores, at the newsstands, and before the television sets. They represented nearly half the workers in offices and spent nearly 80 percent of the consumer dollars in stores. They enjoyed an unprecedented and expanding gender advantage in both national and state elections. . . . Yet so

often in this era, women seemed unaware of the weight and dynamism of their own formidable presence.[11]

It should come as no surprise that women lack cognizance of our own presence, for popular culture works quite hard to keep us in the dark, diverting our energies into fruitless quests for physical beauty, eternal youth, and undying love. It does not have to be this way, for our strength is truly in our numbers if we will work together to envision and create a sane, healthy, and mature humanity. We are at a critical moment in our evolution as women, and much is within our reach. But we cannot afford to be complacent or assume that this change will occur on its own. If we do not walk this hero-path and return the power of our spirit to the world, we will squander our rare and precious chance, and we will have no one to blame but ourselves.

WALKING THE FEMALE HERO-PATH

As we have seen throughout this book, the heroic quest always begins at home in the vast, mysterious landscape of a woman's inner being. No one knows at the outset how long it will last, the kinds of challenges we will face, or how our lives will change as a result. Although allies accompany us each step of the way, only we can move ourselves forward, and only we can choose our directions and the destinations toward which we will head. Occasionally the tracks of a previous quest might help us chart our course, but eventually we must break away and break a new trail, and that is very hard work indeed. What "rules of the road" can guide our steps as we travel the byways of the hero-path?

Perhaps the most important thing to keep in mind is that the heroic quest knows no boundaries of age, gender, race, class, or creed; the "mighty hero of extraordinary powers . . . is each of us . . . not the physical self visible in the mirror, but the [ruler] within."[12] Each journey is designed to unleash that self and bring a deeper level of meaning and vitality to our lives, and no one is excluded from that venture.

But "the quest" is really a misnomer because just as there is no one quester, there is no one quest. The silver horn sounds at many points throughout our lives, challenging whatever holds us in thrall, awakening our great possibilities and desires, inviting us to go where we have never gone before. Each quest is precisely tailored to our maturational needs at any given time, although we may not always feel that this is so. And the more determined a woman is to grow, the more calls to adventure she is certain to receive.

The heroic road is rarely straight and narrow; more often it is full of unexpected twists and turns. So every quester must keep her wits about her and her eyes wide open as she negotiates her route. She must keep her inner muscles supple and strong and dose herself daily with compassion and love. And she must learn to be patient and to wait until the time is right to battle her dragons or launch her transformation or she may exhaust her resources prematurely.

Patience does not mean waiting passively for someone or something to rescue the quester. It means waiting actively, "with the inner certainty of reaching the goal."[13] Every woman who answers the call will transform herself and the world around her, but not all at once, and not always in ways that are visible to the eye. The heroic journey is composed of countless small steps, each of which is vital to the whole. As long as a quester remains true to herself, as long as she does not seek to be rescued or to live through any other human being, as long as she realizes that her own inner strength is the only source on which she can ultimately rely, she will achieve her Grail, no matter how long it takes her to do so.

No one can answer the call to awaken, battle her dragons, or complete a transformation unless she is willing to own her own power. Women often reject the idea of power because we equate it with patriarchal values of domination, exploitation, and control, which have held sway for too many years. But those are merely facets of power masquerading as the whole. Power means the ability to see ourselves clearly, to trust our own instincts and bring our best to birth. It is an ally that bolsters our spirits whenever they flag and helps us survive the rigors of our journeys with our compassion, decency, and humanity intact. As Jean Baker Miller reminds us, power is

the capacity to implement. . . . Women do
not need to diminish other women . . . [or]
take on the destructive attributes which are
not necessarily a part of effective power. . . .
Women need the power to advance their own
development, but they do not "need" the
power to limit the development of others.[14]

Though it may be restating the obvious, heroism
is not synonymous with perfection. We all make many
mistakes on our journeys toward healing and wholeness;
we all fall down and are hurt. Sometimes we make huge
errors of judgment and get bogged down in dreadful
quagmires for extended periods of time. But as painful
as these mistakes may be, they can be ingenious allies of
transformation if we resolve to learn from them and
then move on. As Annie said, "A hero can't be perfect
and be a hero because the word presumes overcoming,
and when you overcome you're not perfect. A hero is
somebody who makes it through whatever she must go
through, who completes her search to the point where
she can truly say, 'I feel okay, and there's more to do.'
Sure she is afraid some of the time, but she has a sense
that by dint of something she can make a difference."

Likewise, heroism isn't hubris. As I learned
through my excursion into death, it is always possible to
take on too much. "Though the terrors will recede before a genuine psychological readiness, the overbold adventurer beyond [her] depth may be shamelessly
undone."[15] Just as a hero must not expect perfection of

herself, so must she develop a deep and healthy appreciation for her very real limits. The female hero-path requires a woman to be her best compass, to use her own inner guidance to discern where she is at any given time. But that compass is useless unless she develops a solid working knowledge of her vocabulary of growth. Depression, illness, panic, fatigue: All can be signposts of healing and change, if only we know how to read them.

Jane has for many years suffered from colitis, an inflammation of the colon which, while painful, provides her with critical information about where she is and what she needs to do. "I feel much of what I absorbed from my religious upbringing tightened my guts; made me over-responsible, over-sensitive, and over-fearful; and ultimately led to colitis. This illness has made me change significantly. If I put too much pressure on myself to accomplish things—usually too many things at once—I tense up my guts, try hard, get everything done, and end up with a colitis attack that can last for a month or more. I am learning to pay attention to the warning pains within me, talk to myself, pull back, relax. I still need to work on this. I think the colitis is making me learn to be a less intense person, to be happier, and to take life as it comes rather than be so controlling. The colitis is transforming me whether I like it or not."

Living heroically requires a woman to live authentically, not recklessly. No one can leap over every tall building; some obstacles are meant to deflect us from paths that would lead to devastation. Sometimes a door closes because it needs to, not because we have done something "wrong." Sometimes something very right is happening even when everything is going awry. Sometimes the most heroic thing a quester can do is stop, turn around, and find another way. Giving way does not mean giving up; it can be, in the words of the I Ching,

> a correct way to behave in order not to exhaust one's forces. . . . Retreat is not to be confused with flight. Flight means saving oneself under any circumstances whereas retreat is a sign of strength. In retreating [one] does not do violence to [one's] convictions.[16]

A quester can discern the difference from the way she feels. If the result of retreat is emptiness, boredom, discontent, or despair, it is a sure sign that she is giving up. But if she feels a sense of rightness and relief even in the midst of disappointment or pain, she is most likely seeking a more congruent direction.

How does a quester know where she's going when she doesn't know where she is? The best way for her to find out is to study her internal road map and read her own clues. This means devoting as much care and attention to her relationship with herself as she gives to others in her life, for it is the strength of this relationship that allows her access to the enormous range of dreams, intuitions, and inner senses we each have at our disposal.

And it is the strength of this relationship that empowers her to walk through the fires of each initiation and emerge a whole person, having found something within herself that only she can contribute to the world.

Yet insight, though essential, is never enough. It must be translated into action and behavior, and that takes perseverance, commitment, and a massive effort of will. It is easy to live the quest when things are going well, but much of the time they're not. Every quester must remember that the journey will be hard, that there will be difficulties and consequences that cannot be foreseen. Sometimes loneliness, anger, fear, and fatigue will threaten to engulf her. Sometimes she will wonder why she ever chose to go on her quest in the first place. Sometimes she will be rejected or ridiculed by family or friends who don't understand what she is attempting to do, and sometimes she must leave them and search for new companions. Sometimes she will feel pressured to hide, turn back, or adjust to the status quo. And sometimes that pressure will come from within, for it may be more difficult to let go of an old self-image than she ever anticipated. As theologian Carol Christ observed,

> For a woman the risk is that when the patriarchal definitions of her being are stripped away, she will be faced with radical freedom; she will have no guidelines to tell her how to act. She must have courage, clear-sightedness, and awareness of the consequences of her choices or she may lose herself.[17]

But we must also remember the consequences of not undertaking a quest; as Abraham Maslow once said, if we deliberately try to be less than our best we'll be desperately unhappy for the rest of our lives.[18] And our world will suffer as well.

The heroic road can be full of suffering, but suffering alone does not a hero make. Ultimately our response to our pain is what matters most. As Zena found, we alone must decide whether to perceive ourselves as victims of circumstances beyond our control or as individuals who are called to discover our depths, resources, and great possibilities and share them with the larger world. And if we choose the latter course, we must pack some essential psychological supplies to sustain us on that journey.

The first of these is humor. A hero must be able to laugh at herself and at the absurdities of life while not succumbing to a belief that either she or her life is absurd. And she must be able to take herself very seriously and, simultaneously, with a grain of salt. As Leah said, "I try to cultivate a sense of humor because I think if I didn't, I would die. The world is so awful that you've got to find what's funny and squeeze all the enjoyment you can out of that. I see this as a very Jewish way of being in the world. Jews have laughed their way through five thousand years, and we're still here. And I find in my Jewish heritage a great deal of strength because, you know, anything can happen. You can't live your life waiting for things to go wrong because they always do eventually. So you live your life and you laugh your laughs, and if something terrible happens, oh well. But at least you will have lived your life."

Emotional flexibility and a commitment to balance are other important psychological tools; they enable a quester to weave together her work, her relationships, and her time for herself in a sane and healthy way. Sarah is an accomplished quilter, a craft she learned during her midlife crisis when she was looking for ways to release her creativity. She selects her colors and designs with exquisite care to capture a mood, a vision, or the essence of the person for whom the quilt is intended. Quilting seems to me a wonderful metaphor for the heroic life; although no one can control every aspect of her internal or external environment, she can live in those environments in an authentic and imaginative way, fitting each experience into the pattern of the whole and finding new ways to express the artistry of her being.

Creating a life that fits the contours of a woman's best self takes an enormous amount of hard and meticulous work because it demands that we live our lives from the inside out on a moment-to-moment basis. Everyone who walks the hero-path must be willing to question everything, challenge everything, live consciously, and speak the truth as she sees it. We must dream our dreams and strive to make them a reality, however great or small those dreams may be. We must follow our paths wherever they lead even when that turns out not to be where we were headed, and we must choose to become the heroes of a myth of our own making.

The heroic quest begins at home, but staying home is not enough. Ultimately we must not only envision and embody a new archetype of heroism but contribute a thousand new faces of heroism to our world. How might we bring this about?

The most powerful gift we can give to each other is the gift of the ally who awakens the quester to her heroic potential. "Wise women initiating younger, questing women are probably more common than available literature, usually researched and written by men, would indicate. However, most myths and accounts portray women, both young and old, offering wisdom to male heroes and creators of various kinds."[19] And so we must recast these tales by assuming the mantle of alliance and offering each other the full force of our wisdom, strength, and love. We must urge our mothers, daughters, sisters, students, colleagues, clients, and friends to consider their experiences from the perspective of the quest, recognizing their moments of awakening and exploring the significance of those moments to the whole of their lives. We must help each other comprehend our periods of initiation as painful but necessary stages on the road toward transformation, shifting our perspective away from passivity and toward the recognition of every woman's capacity to live heroically. And we must believe in each other and the integrity of our quests, empowering, protecting, and guiding each other as we become more fully alive, returning ourselves to ourselves whenever we get lost.

Then we must begin to tell each other the whole

truth about our lives. As mentioned in chapter 1 of this book, most women grow up in silence, rarely hearing the full stories of other women's lives and consequently afraid to reveal many of their own experiences. Few women, even those who have conquered great odds, seem to realize that heroes are made—not born—in the process of grappling with formidable events. But Carolyn Heilbrun reminds us that "Sartre . . . defined the story as freedom confronted by fate, first crushed by misfortunes, then turning against them and gradually controlling them. Genius, he set out to prove, [was] not a gift, but rather the way one invent[ed] in desperate situations."[20] Women must read, hear, and see the stories of other women who have invented themselves in desperate situations to appreciate the profundity of our own lives, to know that we are not alone, and to realize that facing our truth and our pain is a heroic act of strength, not weakness.

There is a great hunger in women for vivid expressions of female strength that traditional symbols of "true womanhood" can never slake. And so our stories must reach far beyond our personal lives and immediate circles of friends, and far beyond the realm of women's studies, literary journals, and professional presentations. As writers, artists, film makers, teachers, poets, musicians, and scholars, we must look into the distorting mirrors of the old, sexist myths and say to the spirits residing there, "Enough."

We must take back our symbols of power and efficacy and refuse to allow them to be used against us.[21]

We must clear new pathways through the ancient wilderness of male supremacy and discard the misogynistic mythological debris. We must unleash the forces of our imagination and wield our creativity with enthusiasm and aplomb. We must build a rich, diverse, and popular literature of female heroism that cherishes and promotes the value of women, reflects the many facets of our being, and explores new ways of relating to life on a personal, community, and planetary level. We must tell the stories of courageous women so we will know that many women in many places throughout the course of time have dreamed "impossible" dreams and made them a reality, and so inspire ourselves to do the same. And we must build models of achievement, justice, and success that wed the reality of power to the ideal of morality and remind us that everyone and everything is a manifestation of the whole.

Perhaps there never was a "golden age" for women, as Bonnie Anderson and Judith Zinsser discovered when they searched the ancient records for stories of women's lives. If such a time ever was, it exists only in our legends of Amazons and Avalon. But we have within us the power, the passion, and the purpose to create that age anew. If we want our voices to be heard, if we want our whole selves reflected in the mirror of consensus reality, if we want to reshape the world along humane, supportive, and responsive dimensions, we must awaken from our deep, protracted sleep and dare to be strong, courageous, and real. We must take firm hold of the reins of the future and choose to act wherever we can, however we can, to bring this quest to birth. And then we must let go of the past and leap across the chasm of change, from where we are to where we have never been before, and go on from there.

Notes

Introduction

1. Carol Pearson and Katherine Pope, *The Female Hero in American and British Literature* (New York: R. R. Bowker Company, 1981).

2. Sarah B. Pomeroy, *Goddesses, Whores, Wives, and Slaves: Women in Classical Antiquity* (New York: Schocken Books, 1975), 102.

3. Ibid., 109.

4. Ibid., 96.

5. Bonnie S. Anderson and Judith P. Zinsser, *A History of Their Own: Women in Europe from Prehistory to the Present*, Vol. 1 (New York: Harper & Row, 1988), 15.

6. Merlin Stone, *When God Was a Woman* (San Diego: Harcourt Brace Jovanovich, 1976), 216.

7. Anderson and Zinsser, *History of Their Own*, 334.

8. Kay Stone, quoted in Marta Weigle, *Spiders and Spinsters* (Albuquerque: University of New Mexico Press, 1982), 208–209.

9. Rhoda Nottridge, *Adventure Films* (New York: Crestwood House, 1992), 11.

10. Julia A. Boyd, "Ethnic and Cultural Diversity: Keys to Power," in Laura S. Brown and Maria P. P. Root, eds., *Diversity and Complexity in Feminist Therapy* (New York: Harrington Park Press, 1990), 151–167.

11. Beverly A. Greene, "What Has Gone Before: The Legacy of Racism and Sexism in the Lives of Black Mothers and Daughters," in Brown and Root, *Diversity and Complexity*, 223.

12. Siew Hwa Beh, "Growing Up with Legends of the Chinese Swordswomen," in Charlene Spretnak, ed., *The Politics of Women's Spirituality: Essays on the Rise of Spiritual Power Within the Feminist Movement* (New York: Doubleday, 1982), 125. See also Judy Yung, "The Social Awakening of Chinese American Women as Reported in Chung Sai Yat Po, 1900–1911," in Ellen C. DuBois and Vicki L. Ruiz, eds., *Unequal Sisters: A Multi-Cultural Reader in U.S. Women's History* (New York: Routledge, 1990), 195–207.

13. Rayna Green, "The Pocahontas Perplex: The Image of Indian Women in American Culture," in DuBois and Ruiz, *Unequal Sisters*, 19.

14. Nottridge, *Adventure Films*, 29.

15. Sarah B. Pomeroy, *Goddesses, Whores, Wives, and Slaves*, 96.

16. Carolyn G. Heilbrun, *Writing A Woman's Life* (New York: W. W. Norton & Company, 1988; Ballantine, 1989), 131.

CHAPTER ONE—THE JOURNEY BEGINS

1. Ethel Johnston Phelps, *The Maid of the North: Feminist Folk Tales from around the World* (New York: Henry Holt and Company, 1981), 40.

2. Joseph Campbell, *The Power of Myth* (New York: Doubleday, 1988), xviii.

3. Merlin Stone, *When God Was a Woman* (San Diego: Harcourt Brace Jovanovich, 1976).

4. Jean Shinoda Bolen, *Goddesses in Everywoman: A New Psychology of Women* (San Francisco: Harper & Row, 1984).

5. Clarissa Pinkola Estes, *Women Who Run with the Wolves: Myths and Stories of the Wild Woman Archetype* (New York: Ballantine Books, 1992).

6. Elaine Pagels, *Adam, Eve, and the Serpent* (New York, Random House, 1988).

7. Fatima Mernissi, *The Veil and the Male Elite: A Feminist Interpretation of Women's Rights in Islam* (Reading: Addison-Wesley Publishing Company, 1991).

8. Barbara G. Walker, *The Woman's Dictionary of Symbols and Sacred Objects* (San Francisco: HarperCollins, 1988).

9. Joseph Campbell, *The Hero with a Thousand Faces* (Princeton: Princeton University Press, 1949).

10. Ibid., 116.

11. Charlene Spretnak, ed., *The Politics of Women's Spirituality: Essays on the Rise of Spiritual Power within the Feminist Movement* (New York: Doubleday, 1982), 90.

12. See, for example, Martha A. Ackelsberg, *Free Women of Spain: Anarchism and the Struggle for the Emancipation of Women* (Bloomington: Indiana University Press, 1991); Bonnie S. Anderson and Judith P. Zinsser, *A History of Their Own: Women in Europe from Prehistory to the Present*, vols. 1 and 2 (New York: Harper & Row, 1988); Anne Cameron, *Daughters of Copper Woman* (Vancouver: Press Gang Publishers, 1981); Nien Cheng, *Life and Death in Shanghai* (New York: Penguin Books, 1986); Judy Chicago, "Our Heritage Is Our Power," in Spretnak, *Politics and Women's Spirituality*; Jill Ker Conway, *The Road from Coorain* (New York: Vintage

Books, 1989); Vivian Cornick and Barbara K. Moran, eds., *Women in Sexist Society: Studies in Power and Powerlessness* (New York: New American Library, 1971); William Drake, *The First Wave: Women Poets in America (1915–1945)* (New York: Macmillan Publishing Company, 1987); Ellen C. DuBois and Vicki L. Ruiz, eds., *Unequal Sisters: A Multi-Cultural Reader in Women's History* (New York: Routledge, 1990); Antonia Fraser, *The Warrior Queens* (New York: Vintage Books, 1988); Joline Godfrey, *Our Wildest Dreams: Women Entrepreneurs Making Money, Having Fun, Doing Good* (New York: Harper Business, 1992); Evelyn Fox Keller, *A Feeling for the Organism: The Life and Work of Barbara McClintock* (New York: W. H. Freeman and Company, 1983); Gerda Lerner, ed., *Black Women in White America: A Documentary History* (New York: Vintage Books, 1972); Sarah L. Lightfoot, *Balm in Gilead: Journey of a Healer* (New York: Addison-Wesley Publishing Company, 1988); Ann L. Macdonald, *Feminine Ingenuity: Women and Invention in America* (New York: Ballantine Books, 1991); Rigoberta Menchu, *I, Rigoberta Menchu: An Indian Woman in Guatemala*, trans. Ann Wright (London: Verson, 1984); Fatima Mernissi, *Beyond the Veil: Male-Female Dynamics in Modern Muslim Society* (Bloomington: Indiana University Press, 1987); Mei Nakano, *Japanese American Women: Three Generations 1908–1990* (Berkeley: Mina Press, 1990); Daphne Patai, *Brazilian Women Speak: Contemporary Life Stories* (New Brunswick: Rutgers University Press, 1988); Phyllis J. Read and Bernard L. Witlieb, *The Book of Women's Firsts: Breakthrough Achievements of Almost 1000 Women . . .* (New York: Random House, 1992); Barbara Sapinsley, *The Private War of Mrs. Packard* (New York: Paragon House, 1991); Linda K. Silverman, "It All Began with Leta Hollingworth," *Journal for the Education of the Gifted* 12, no. 2 (1989): 86–98; Emilie Smith-Ayala, *The Granddaughters of Ixmucane: Guatemalan*

Women Speak (Toronto: Women's Press, 1991); Barbara Solomon, *In the Company of Educated Women* (New Haven: Yale University Press, 1985); Gloria Steinem, *Outrageous Acts and Everyday Rebellions* (New York: New American Library, 1983); Marilyn Waring, *If Women Counted: A New Feminist Economics* (San Francisco: Harper San Francisco, 1988); Howard Zinn, *A People's History of the United States* (New York: Harper Perennial, 1980).

13. Anderson and Zinsser, *History of Their Own* 2:192.

14. Jean Baker Miller, *Toward a New Psychology of Women* (Boston: Beacon Press, 1976, 1986), 10–17.

15. Kathleen D. Noble, "The Dilemma of the Gifted Woman," *Psychology of Women Quarterly* 11 (1987): 367–378; "Counseling Gifted Women: Becoming the Heroes of Our Own Lives," *Journal for the Education of the Gifted* 12 (1989): 131–141; "Living Out the Promise of High Potential: Perceptions of 100 Gifted Women," *Advanced Development Journal* 1 (1989): 57–75.

16. See, for example, Barbara Clark, *Growing Up Gifted: Developing the Potential of Children at Home and at School* (Columbus: Charles E. Merrill Publishing Company, 1983); and Linda K. Silverman, "What Happens to the Gifted Girl?" in C. J. Maker, ed., *Defensible Programs for the Gifted* (Rockville: Aspen, 1986), 43–89.

17. Carolyn G. Heilbrun, *Writing a Woman's Life* (New York: W. W. Norton & Co., 1988; Ballantine, 1989), 97–98.

18. Carol Gilligan, Nona P. Lyons, and Trudy J. Hanmer, eds., *Making Connections: The Relational Worlds of Adolescent Girls at Emma Willard School* (Cambridge: Harvard University Press, 1990).

19. Emily Hancock, *The Girl Within* (New York: Fawcett Columbine, 1989).

20. Campbell, *Hero with a Thousand Faces*, 25.

CHAPTER TWO—THE CALL TO AWAKEN

1. Joseph Campbell, *The Power of Myth* (New York: Doubleday, 1988), 129.
2. Joseph Campbell, *The Hero with a Thousand Faces* (Princeton: Princeton University Press, 1949), 51.
3. Ibid., 64.
4. Jesus to Thomas, quoted by Elaine Pagels in *The Gnostic Gospels* (New York: Vintage Books, 1979), xiii–xiv.

CHAPTER THREE—THE DRAGONS OF INITIATION

1. Carol Pearson and Katherine Pope, *The Female Hero in American and British Literature* (New York: R. R. Bowker Company, 1981), 70.
2. Omar Khayyám, *Rubáiyát*, trans. E. Fitzgerald (Mount Vernon: Peter Pauper Press, 1953), 40.
3. See, for example, John Bowlby, *Attachment and Loss*, 3 vols. (New York: Basic Books, 1969; 1973; 1980); Laura S. Brown and Maria P. P. Root, eds., *Diversity and Complexity in Feminist Therapy* (New York: Harrington Park Press, 1990); Phyllis Chesler, *Women and Madness* (San Diego: Harcourt Brace Jovanovich, 1972, 1989); Vivian Cornick and Barbara K. Moran, eds., *Woman in Sexist Society: Studies in Power and Powerlessness* (New York: New American Library, 1971); J. Garber & M. E. P. Seligman, eds., *Human Helplessness* (New York: Academic, 1980); Alice Miller, *The Drama of the Gifted Child* (New York: Basic Books, 1981); Jean Baker Miller, *Toward a New Psychology of Women* (Boston: Beacon Press, 1976, 1986); Kathleen D. Noble, "The Dilemma of the Gifted Woman," *Psychology of Women Quarterly* 11 (1987): 367–378; Maggie Scharf, *Unfinished Business: Pressure Points in the Lives of Women* (New York: Doubleday, 1980); Judith Viorst, *Necessary Losses* (New York: Fawcett, 1987); Lenore E.

Walker, *The Battered Woman* (New York: Harper & Row, 1979).

4. Sally M. Reis and Carolyn M. Callahan, "Gifted Females: They've Come a Long Way—Or Have They?" *Journal for the Education of the Gifted* 12, no. 2 (1989): 99–117.

5. Lee Anne Bell, "Something's Wrong Here and It's Not Me: Challenging the Dilemmas That Block Girls' Success," *Journal for the Education of the Gifted* 12, no. 2 (1989): 118–130.

6. Carolyn G. Heilbrun, *Writing a Woman's Life* (New York: W. W. Norton & Company, 1988; Ballantine, 1989), 130.

7. Naomi Wolf, *The Beauty Myth: How Images of Beauty Are Used against Women* (New York: William Morrow, 1991; Doubleday Anchor, 1992).

8. Harriet Goldhor Lerner, *The Dance of Anger* (New York: Harper & Row, 1985).

9. Ibid., 2.

10. Barbara A. Kerr, *Smart Girls, Gifted Women* (Columbus: Ohio Psychology Publishing Company, 1985).

11. Ibid., 70.

12. Carol S. Dweck and Barbara G. Licht, "Learned Helplessness and Intellectual Achievement," in Garber and Seligman, *Human Helplessness*.

13. Kathleen D. Noble, "Living Out the Promise of High Potential: Perceptions of 100 Gifted Women," *Advanced Development Journal* 1 (1989): 57–75.

14. Norman Garmezy and Auke Tellegen, "Studies of Stress-Resistant Children: Methods, Variables, and Preliminary Findings," in F. J. Morrison, C. Lord, and D. P. Keating, eds., *Applied Developmental Psychology* (Orlando: Academic, 1984).

15. Abraham H. Maslow, *Religions, Values, and Peak Experiences* (New York: Penguin Books, 1970).

16. Kathleen D. Noble, "Psychological Health and the

Experience of Transcendence," *The Counseling Psychologist* 15, no. 4 (1987): 601–614.

17. See, for example, Andrew M. Greeley, *Ecstasy: A Way of Knowing* (Englewood Cliffs: Prentice-Hall, 1974); William James, *The Varieties of Religious Experience* (New York: Modern Library, 1902); Kathleen D. Noble, (ibid); Kenneth Ring, *Heading toward Omega: In Search of the Meaning of the Near-Death Experience* (New York: William Morrow, 1984); Roger Walsh and Dean H. Shapiro, Jr., *Beyond Health and Normality: Explorations of Exceptional Psychological Well-Being* (New York: Van Nostrand Reinhold, 1983); John White, ed., *The Highest State of Consciousness* (New York: Anchor Books, 1972).

18. Viorst, *Necessary Losses.*

19. Jessie Bernard, "The Inferiority Curriculum," *Psychology of Women Quarterly* 12, no. 3 (1988): 265.

20. Pearson and Pope, *Female Hero*, 8.

CHAPTER FOUR—ALLIES OF ALL SEASONS

1. Carol Pearson and Katherine Pope, *The Female Hero in American and British Literature* (New York: R. R. Bowker Company, 1981), 84.

2. Ibid., 83.

3. Phyllis Chesler, *Women and Madness* (San Diego: Harcourt Brace Jovanovich, 1972, 1989).

4. See, for example, Laura S. Brown and Maria P. P. Root, eds., *Diversity and Complexity in Feminist Therapy* (New York: Harrington Park Press, 1990); Carol P. Christ, *Diving Deep and Surfacing: Women Writers on Spiritual Quest* (Boston: Beacon Press, 1980); Carol Gilligan, *In a Different Voice: Psychological Theory and Women's Development* (Cambridge: Harvard University Press, 1982); Carolyn G. Heilbrun, *Writing a Woman's Life* (New York: W. W. Norton

& Company, 1988; Ballantine, 1989); Mary F. Belenky et al., *Women's Ways of Knowing: The Development of Self, Voice, and Mind* (New York: Basic Books, 1986); Jean Baker Miller, *Toward a New Psychology of Women* (Boston: Beacon Press, 1976, 1986).

CHAPTER FIVE—TRANSFORMATION AND RETURN

1. Adrienne Rich, "Prospective Immigrants Please Note," in *Collected Early Poems, 1950–1970* (New York: W. W. Norton & Company, 1993), 188.

2. Viktor E. Frankl, *Man's Search for Meaning: An Introduction to Logotherapy* (New York: Simon & Schuster, 1959, 1963).

3. Carolyn G. Heilbrun, *Writing a Woman's Life* (New York: W. W. Norton & Company, 1988; Ballantine, 1989), 39.

4. Carol Pearson and Katherine Pope, *The Female Hero in American and British Literature* (New York: R. R. Bowker Company, 1981), 103.

5. T. S. Eliot, "Little Gidding, The Four Quartets," in *Collected Poems, 1909–1962.* (San Diego: Harcourt Brace Jovanovich, 1930, 1984), 208.

6. Joseph Campbell, *The Power of Myth* (New York: Doubleday, 1988), 193.

7. Ibid., xv.

8. Sarah Lawrence Lightfoot, *Balm in Gilead: Journey of a Healer* (New York: Addison-Wesley Publishing Company, 1988), 306.

CHAPTER SIX—TOWARD A NEW MYTHOLOGY OF HEROISM

1. Susan Faludi, *Backlash* (New York: Crown Publishers, 1991; Doubleday Anchor, 1992), 458.

2. Carol Pearson and Katherine Pope, *The Female Hero in American and British Literature* (New York: R. R. Bowker Company, 1981), 176.

3. Quoted in Pearson and Pope, *Female Hero*, 252.

4. John Matthews, ed., *At the Table of the Grail: Magic and the Use of the Imagination* (London: Routledge & Kegan Paul, 1984).

5. Hannah Closs, "The Meeting of the Waters," in Matthews, *Table of the Grail*, 29–48.

6. Roger Sherman Loomis, *The Grail: From Celtic Myth to Christian Symbol* (New Jersey: Princeton University Press, 1963, 1991).

7. See, for example, Helen Adolph, *Visio Pacis: Holy City and Grail* (Pennsylvania: Pennsylvania State University Press, 1960); and Emma Jung and Marie-Louise Von Franz, *The Grail Legend*, trans. Andrea Dykes (Boston: Sigo Press, 1986).

8. Barbara G. Walker, *The Woman's Encyclopedia of Myths and Secrets* (San Francisco, HarperCollins, 1983).

9. Joseph Campbell, *The Power of Myth* (New York: Doubleday, 1988), 25.

10. Carol P. Christ, *Diving Deep and Surfacing: Women Writers on Spiritual Quest* (Boston: Beacon Press, 1980), 8.

11. Faludi, *Backlash*, 458.

12. Joseph Campbell, *The Hero with a Thousand Faces* (Princeton: Princeton University Press, 1949), 365.

13. *The I Ching or Book of Changes*, trans. Richard Wilhelm and Cary F. Baynes (Princeton: Princeton University Press, 1950), 24.

14. Jean Baker Miller, *Toward a New Psychology of Women* (Boston: Beacon Press, 1976, 1986), 117.

15. Campbell, *Hero with a Thousand Faces*, 84.

16. *I Ching*, 129–130.

17. Christ, *Diving Deep*, 31.

18. Abraham Maslow, *The Farther Reaches of Human Nature* (New York: Penguin Books, 1982).

19. Marta Weigle, *Spiders and Spinsters* (Albuquerque: University of New Mexico Press, 1982), 129.

20. Carolyn G. Heilbrun, *Writing a Woman's Life* (New York: W. W. Norton & Company 1988; Ballantine, 1989), 44.

21. The ancient word *virgin*, for example, originally denoted an unmarried priestess who healed, prophesied, performed sacred dances, and "dispensed the Mother's grace through sexual worship," not a woman whose sexuality was regulated by men. See Barbara G. Walker, *The Woman's Encyclopedia of Myths and Secrets* (San Francisco: HarperCollins, 1983), 1049. In the seventeenth century, Catherine de Vivonne invented the salon as a space where intellectually oriented women could meet with men as their equals. Her idea caught hold and spread rapidly throughout Europe, and by the early eighteenth century the word *bluestocking* had been coined to describe scholarly women who attended such salons in England. But some fifty years later a backlash occurred, and the word was used to derogate any woman who aspired to learning. See Bonnie Anderson and Judith Zinsser, *A History of Their Own*, vol. 2 (New York: Harper & Row, 1988), 103–128. Lest we think that such a thing could happen only in the distant past, we have only to regard the fate of the term *feminist*. This word was introduced by Hubertine Auclert in the late nineteenth century to promote civil rights for women, but it was so maligned by forces opposed to the women's movement in the twentieth century that many women are now embarrassed to describe themselves as such. See the discussion of "Backlashes Then and Now" in Faludi, *Backlash*, 46–72.

Selected
Bibliography

Ackelsberg, M. A. *Free Women of Spain: Anarchism and the Struggle for the Emancipation of Women.* Bloomington: Indiana University Press, 1991.

Adolph, H. *Visio Pacis: Holy City and Grail.* Pennsylvania: Pennsylvania State University Press, 1960.

Anderson, B. S., and J. P. Zinsser. *A History of Their Own: Women in Europe from Prehistory to the Present.* 2 vols. New York: Harper & Row, 1988.

Belenky, M. F., B. M. Clinchy, N. R. Goldberger, and J. M. Tarule. *Women's Ways of Knowing: The Development of Self, Voice, and Mind.* New York: Basic Books, 1986.

Bell, E. S. "The Women Flyers: From Aviatrix to Astronaut." In *Heroines of Popular Culture,* edited by P. Browne, 54–62. Bowling Green: Bowling Green State University Popular Press, 1987.

Bell, L. A. "Something's Wrong Here and It's Not Me: Challenging the Dilemmas that Block Girls' Success." *Journal for the Education of the Gifted* 12, no. 2 (1989): 118–130.

Bernal, M. *Black Athena: The Afroasiatic Roots of Classical*

Civilization. New Brunswick: Rutgers University Press, 1987.

Bernard, J. "The Inferiority Curriculum," *Psychology of Women Quarterly* 12, no. 3 (1988).

Bohan, J. S. "Contextual History: A Framework for Replacing Women in the History of Psychology." *Psychology of Women Quarterly* 14, no. 2 (1990): 213–227.

Bolen, J. S. *Goddesses in Everywoman: A New Psychology of Women.* San Francisco: Harper & Row, 1984.

Bowlby, J. *Attachment and Loss.* 3 vols. New York: Basic Books, 1969, 1973, 1980.

Boyd, J. A. "Ethnic and Cultural Diversity: Keys to Power." In *Diversity and Complexity in Feminist Therapy,* edited by L. S. Brown and M. P. P. Root, 151–167. New York: Harrington Park Press, 1990.

Braxton, J., and A. N. McLaughlin, eds. *Wild Women in the Whirlwind: Afra-American Culture and the Contemporary Literary Renaissance.* New Brunswick: Rutgers University Press, 1990.

Brown, E. B. "Womanist Consciousness: Maggie Lena Walker and the Independent Order of Saint Luke." In *Unequal Sisters: A Multi-Cultural Reader in U.S. Women's History,* edited by E. C. Dubois and V. L. Ruiz, 208–223. New York: Routledge, 1990.

Brown, L. S. "Women, Weight, and Power: Feminist Theoretical and Therapeutic Issues." *Women & Therapy* 4, no. 1 (1985): 61–71.

Brown, L. S., and M. P. P. Root, eds. *Diversity and Complexity in Feminist Therapy.* New York: Harrington Park Press, 1990.

Browne, P., ed. *Heroines of Popular Culture.* Bowling Green: Bowling Green State University Popular Press, 1987.

Cameron, A. *Daughters of Copper Woman.* Vancouver: Press Gang Publishers, 1981.

Campbell, J. *The Hero with a Thousand Faces*. Princeton: Princeton University Press, 1949.

———. *The Power of Myth*. New York: Doubleday, 1988.

Cheng, N. *Life and Death in Shanghai*. New York: Penguin Books, 1986.

Chesler, P. *Women and Madness*. San Diego: Harcourt Brace Jovanovich, 1972, 1989.

———. "The Amazon Legacy." In *The Politics of Women's Spirituality*, edited by C. Spretnak, 97–113. New York: Doubleday, 1982.

Chicago, J. "Our Heritage Is Our Power." In *The Politics of Women's Spirituality*, edited by C. Spretnak, 152–156. New York: Doubleday, 1982.

Christ, C. P. *Diving Deep and Surfacing: Women Writers on Spiritual Quest*. Boston: Beacon Press, 1980.

Clark, B. *Growing Up Gifted: Developing the Potential of Children at Home and at School*. Columbus: Charles E. Merrill Publishing Company, 1983.

Closs, H. "The Meeting of the Waters." In *At the Table of the Grail: Magic and the Use of the Imagination*, edited by John Matthews, 29–48. London: Routledge & Kegan Paul, 1984.

Conway, J. K. *The Road from Coorain*. New York: Vintage Books, 1990.

Drake, W. *The First Wave: Women Poets in America (1915–1945)*. New York: Macmillan Publishing Company, 1987.

Drinker, S. "The Origins of Music: Women's Goddess Worship." In *The Politics of Women's Spirituality*, edited by C. Spretnak, 39–48. New York: Doubleday, 1982.

Dubois, E. C., and V. L. Ruiz, eds. *Unequal Sisters: A Multi-Cultural Reader in U. S. Women's History*. New York: Routledge, 1990.

Dweck, C. S., and B. G. Licht. "Learned Helplessness and Intellectual Achievement." In *Human Helplessness*, edited by J. Garber and M. E. P. Seligman, 197–221. New York: Academic, 1980.

El-Saadawi, Nawal. *Two Women in One*. Trans. by Osman Nusairi and Jana Gough. Seattle: Seal Press, 1986.

Eliot, T. S. "Little Gidding, The Four Quartets." In *Collected Poems, 1909–1962*. San Diego: Harcourt Brace Jovanovich, 1930, 1984.

Estes, C. P. *Women Who Run with the Wolves: Myths and Stories of the Wild Woman Archetype*. New York: Ballantine Books, 1992.

Faludi, S. *Backlash: The Undeclared War against American Women*. New York: Crown Publishers, 1991.

Frankl, V. E. *Man's Search for Meaning: An Introduction to Logotherapy*. New York: Simon & Schuster, 1959, 1963.

Fraser, A. *The Warrior Queens*. New York: Vintage Books, 1988.

Garber, J., and M. E. P. Seligman. *Human Helplessness*. New York: Academic, 1980.

Garmezy, N., and A. Tellegen. "Studies of Stress-Resistant Children: Methods, Variables, and Preliminary Findings." In *Applied Developmental Psychology*, edited by F. J. Morrison, C. Lord, and D. P. Keating, 231–283. Orlando: Academic, 1984.

Gilligan, C. *In a Different Voice: Psychological Theory and Women's Development*. Cambridge: Harvard University Press, 1982.

Gilligan, C., N. P. Lyons, and T. J. Hanmer, eds. *The Relational World of Adolescent Girls at Emma Willard School*. Cambridge: Harvard University Press, 1990.

Gornick, V., and B. K. Moran, eds. *Woman in Sexist Society: Studies in Power and Powerlessness*. New York: New American Library, 1971.

Greeley, A. *Ecstasy: A Way of Knowing*. Englewood Cliffs: Prentice-Hall, 1974.

Green, R. "The Pocahontas Perplex: The Image of Indian Women in American Culture." In *Unequal Sisters: A Multi-Cultural Reader in U.S. Women's History,* edited by E. D. Dubois and V. L. Ruiz, 15–21. New York: Routledge, 1990.

Greene, B. A. "What Has Gone Before: The Legacy of Racism and Sexism in the Lives of Black Mothers and Daughters." In *Diversity and Complexity in Feminist Therapy,* edited by L. S. Brown and M. P. P. Root, 207–230. New York: Harrington Park Press, 1990.

Hancock, E. *The Girl Within.* New York: Fawcett Columbine, 1989.

Heilbrun, C. G. *Writing a Woman's Life.* New York: W. W. Norton & Company, 1988.

The I Ching or Book of Changes. Trans. by Richard Wilhelm and Cary F. Baynes. Princeton: Princeton University Press, 1950.

James, W. *The Varieties of Religious Experience.* New York: Modern Library, 1902.

Jung, E., and M-L Franz. *The Grail Legend.* Trans. by Andrea Dykes. Boston: Sigo Press, 1986.

Keller, E. F. *A Feeling for the Organism: The Life and Work of Barbara McClintock.* New York: W. H. Freeman and Co., 1983.

Kerr, B. *Smart Girls, Gifted Women.* Columbus: Ohio Psychology Publishing Company, 1985.

Khayyám, O. *Rubáiyát.* Trans. by E. Fitzgerald. New York: Peter Pauper Press, 1953.

Lerner, G. *Black Women in White America: A Documentary History.* New York: Vintage Books, 1972.

———. *The Creation of Patriarchy.* New York: Oxford University Press, 1986.

Lerner, H. G. *The Dance of Anger.* New York: Harper & Row, 1985.

Lightfoot, S. L. *Balm in Gilead: Journey of a Healer.* New York: Addison-Wesley Publishing Company, 1988.

Loomis, R. S. *The Grail: From Celtic Myth to Christian Symbol.* Princeton: Princeton University Press, 1963, 1991.

Macdonald, A. L. *Feminine Ingenuity: Woman and Invention in America.* New York: Ballantine Books, 1992.

Maslow, A. H. *Religions, Values, and Peak Experiences.* New York: Penguin Books, 1970.

——. *The Farther Reaches of Human Nature.* New York: Penguin Books., 1972.

Matthews, J., ed. *At the Table of the Grail: Magic and the Use of the Imagination.* London: Routledge & Kegan Paul, 1984.

Menchu, R. *I, Rigoberta Menchu: An Indian Woman in Guatemala.* Trans. by Ann Wright. London: Verson, 1984.

Mernissi, F. *Beyond the Veil: Male-Female Dynamics in Modern Muslim Society.* Bloomington: Indiana University Press, 1987.

——. *The Veil and the Male Elite: A Feminist Interpretation of Women's Rights in Islam.* Reading: Addison-Wesley Publishing Company, 1991.

Miller, A. *The Drama of the Gifted Child.* New York: Basic Books, 1981.

Miller, J. B. *Toward a New Psychology of Women.* Boston: Beacon Press, 1986.

Nakano, M. *Japanese American Women: Three Generations 1890-1990.* Berkeley: Mina Press Publishing, 1990.

Noble, K. D. "The Dilemma of the Gifted Woman." *Psychology of Women Quarterly* 11 (1987): 367-378.

——. "Psychological Health and the Experience of Transcendence." *The Counseling Psychologist* 15, no. 4 (1987): 601-614.

——. "Counseling Gifted Women: Becoming the Heroes of Our Own Lives." *Journal for the Education of the Gifted* 12, no. 2 (1989): 131-141.

———. "Living Out the Promise of High Potential: Perceptions of 100 Gifted Women." *Advanced Development Journal* 1 (1989): 57–75.

Nochlin, L. "Why Are There No Great Women Artists?" In *Woman in Sexist Society: Studies in Power and Powerlessness*, edited by V. Gornick and B. K. Moran, 480–509. New York: New American Library, 1971.

Pagels, E. *The Gnostic Gospels*. New York: Vintage Books, 1979.

———. *Adam, Eve, and the Serpent*. New York: Random House, 1988.

Patai, D. *Brazilian Women Speak: Contemporary Life Stories*. New Brunswick: Rutgers University Press, 1988.

Pearson, C., and K. Pope. *The Female Hero in American and British Literature*. New York: R. R. Bowker Co., 1981.

Phelps, E. J. *The Maid of the North: Feminist Fairy Tales from around the World*. New York: Henry Holt and Company, 1981.

Pomeroy, S. B. *Goddesses, Whores, Wives, and Slaves*. New York: Schocken Books, 1975.

Reis, S. M., and C. M. Callahan. "Gifted Females: They've Come a Long Way—Or Have They?" *Journal for the Education of the Gifted* 12, no. 2 (1989): 99–117.

Rich, A. "Prepatriarchal Female/Goddess Images." In *The Politics of Women's Spirituality*, edited by C. Spretnak, 32–38. New York: Doubleday, 1982.

———. *Collected Early Poems, 1950–1970*. New York: W. W. Norton & Company, 1993.

Ring, K. *Heading toward Omega: In Search of the Meaning of Near-Death Experience*. New York: William Morrow, 1984.

Rodenstein, J., L. Pfleger, and N. Colangelo. "Career Development of Gifted Women." *Gifted Child Quarterly* 21, no. 3 (1977): 383–390.

Ruiz, V. L. "A Promise Fulfilled: Mexican Cannery Workers

in Southern California." In *Unequal Sisters: A Multi-Cultural Reader in U.S. Women's History*, edited by E. D. Dubois and V. L. Ruiz, 264–274. New York: Routledge, 1990.

Sapinsley, B. *The Private War of Mrs. Packard.* New York: Paragon House, 1991.

Scarf, M. *Unfinished Business: Pressure Points in the Lives of Women.* New York: Doubleday, 1980.

Siew, Hwa Beh. "Growing Up with Legends of the Chinese Swordswomen." In *The Politics of Women's Spirituality*, edited by C. Spretnak, 121–126. New York: Doubleday, 1982.

Silverman, L. K. "What Happens to the Gifted Girl?" In *Defensible Programs for the Gifted*, edited by C. J. Maker, 43–89. Rockville: Aspen, 1986.

———. "It All Began with Leta Hollingworth: The Story of Giftedness in Women." *Journal for the Education of the Gifted* 12, no. 2 (1989): 86–98.

Smith-Ayala, E. *The Granddaughters of Ixmucane: Guatemalan Women Speak.* Toronto: Women's Press, 1991.

Sojourner, S. "From the House of Yemanja: The Goddess Heritage of Black Women." In *The Politics of Women's Spirituality*, edited by C. Spretnak, 57–63. New York: Doubleday, 1982.

Solomon, B. M. *In the Company of Educated Women.* New Haven: Yale University Press, 1985.

Spretnak, C., ed. *The Politics of Women's Spirituality: Essays on the Rise of Spiritual Power Within the Feminist Movement.* New York: Doubleday, 1982.

Steinem, G. "Tales of a Reincarnated Amazon Princess: The Invincible Wonder Woman." In *The Politics of Women's Spirituality*, edited by C. Spretnak, 114–120. New York: Doubleday, 1982.

———. *Outrageous Acts and Everyday Rebellions.* New York: New American Library, 1983.

Stone, M. *When God Was a Woman*. San Diego: Harcourt Brace Jovanovich, 1978.

Viorst, Judith. *Necessary Losses*. New York: Fawcett, 1987.

Walker, B. G. *The Woman's Encyclopedia of Myths and Secrets*. San Francisco: Harper & Row, 1983.

———. *The Woman's Dictionary of Symbols and Sacred Objects*. San Francisco: HarperCollins, 1988.

Walker, L. *The Battered Woman*. New York: Harper & Row, 1979.

Walsh, R., and D. H. Shapiro, Jr., eds. *Beyond Health and Normality: Explorations of Exceptional Psychological Well-Being*. New York: Van Nostrand Reinhold, 1983.

Weigle, M. *Spiders and Spinsters: Women and Mythology*. Albuquerque: University of New Mexico Press, 1982.

White, J., ed. *The Highest State of Consciousness*. New York: Anchor Books, 1972.

Wolf, N. *The Beauty Myth: How Images of Beauty Are Used against Women*. New York: William Morrow, 1991.

Wylie, W. *Collected Poems*. New York: Alfred A. Knopf, 1938.

Yung, J. "The Social Awakening of Chinese American Women as Reported in Chung Sai Yat Po, 1900–1911." In *Unequal Sisters: A Multi-Cultural Reader in U.S. Women's History*, edited by E. D. Dubois and V. L. Ruiz, 195–207. New York: Routledge, 1990.

Zinn, H. *A People's History of the United States*. New York: Harper Perennial, 1980.

Zipes, J., ed. *Don't Bet on the Prince: Contemporary Feminist Fairy Tales in North America and England*. New York: Methuen, 1986.

About the Author

Kathleen Noble received her doctorate in counseling psychology in 1984 from the University of Washington, where she is currently a Research Assistant Professor of Women Studies and the Assistant Director of the Halbert Robinson Center for the Study of Capable Youth. Dr. Noble is also a practicing psychologist in Seattle. She has authored and co-authored numerous scholarly papers about highly capable children and adults. This is her first book.